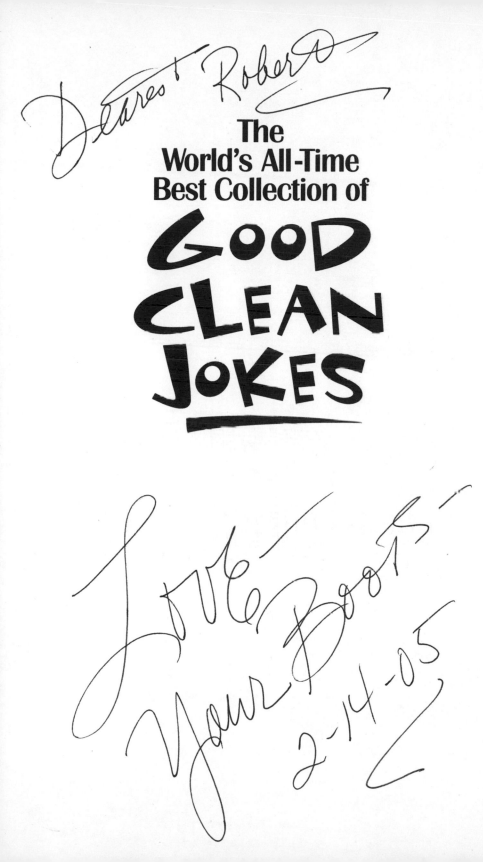

Dearest Robert

The
World's All-Time
Best Collection of

GOOD
CLEAN
JOKES

Love

Your Boots

2-14-05

The World's All-Time Best Collection of

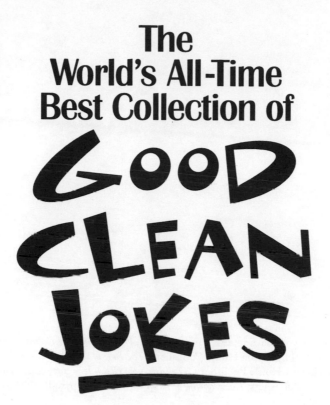

GOOD CLEAN JOKES

Bob Phillips

GALAHAD BOOKS
NEW YORK

First Galahad Books edition published in 1996.

Galahad Books
A division of BBS Publishing Corporation
386 Park Avenue South
New York, NY 10016

Galahad Books is a registered trademark of BBS Publishing Corporation.

Published by arrangement with Harvest House Publishers.

Library of Congress Catalog Card Number: 96-77054
ISBN: 0-88365-967-0

Printed in the United States of America.

The World's All-Time Best Collection of

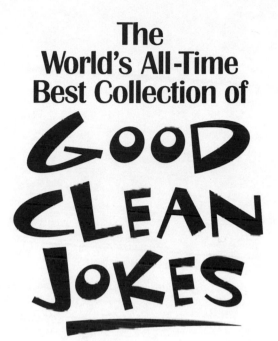

GOOD
CLEAN
JOKES

A

Above Average

Wife: Scientists claim that the average person speaks ten thousand words a day.

Husband: Yes, dear, but remember you are far above the average.

Absentminded

I'm getting so absentminded that sometimes in the middle of a sentence I . . .

Accident

Policeman: How did this accident happen?

Motorist: My wife fell asleep in the backseat.

An insurance claim agent was teaching his wife to drive when the brakes suddenly failed on a steep, downhill grade.

"I can't stop!" she shrilled. "What should I do?"

"Brace yourself," advised her husband, "and try to hit something cheap."

Driving instructor: What would you do if you were going up an icy hill and the motor stalled and the brakes failed?

Student: I'd quickly adjust the rearview mirror.

"Pull over to the curb," said the policeman. "You don't have a tail-light."

The motorist stepped out, looked in back of the car, and stood quivering and speechless. "Oh, it's not that bad," said the policeman.

The man mumbled, "It's not the taillight I'm worried about. Where is my wife and trailer?"

∽⊖—⊖∾

A lady driving along hit a guy. She yelled, "Watch out!"

He said, "Why? Are you coming back?"

∽⊖—⊖∾

A man walking along the road saw an Indian lying with his ear to the ground. He went over and listened. The Indian said, "Large wheels, Ford pickup truck, green color, man driving with large police dog next to him, Colorado license plate and traveling about 75 miles per hour."

The man was astounded. "You mean you can tell all that just by listening with your ear to the ground?" he said.

"Ear to the ground, nothing," said the Indian. "That truck just ran over me."

∽⊖—⊖∾

Wife: Honey, I can't get the car started. I think it's flooded.
Husband: Where is it?
Wife: In the swimming pool.
Husband: It's flooded.

Aches and Pains

I've got so many aches and pains that if a new one comes today, it will be at least two weeks before I can worry about it.

∽⊖—⊖∾

People who cough incessantly never seem to go to a doctor—they go to banquets, concerts, and church.

∽⊖—⊖∾

Two women went to the movies and one of them started to cough. Her friend leaned away from her. The more she coughed, the farther her friend tried to move away. Finally, the cougher turned around to her friend and said, "Look, you don't have to move away like that. This is not a sickness." Her friend replied, "Well, it isn't a wellness."

❧—☙

A man rushed into a drugstore and asked a pharmacist for something to stop hiccups. The druggist poured a glass of water and threw it into the man's face.

"Why did you do that?" the man exploded angrily.

"Well, you don't have hiccups now, do you?"

"No!" shouted the customer. "But my wife out in the car still does!"

❧—☙

You have two chances: one of getting the germ, and one of not getting the germ. If you get the germ, you have two chances: one of getting the disease, and one of not getting the disease. If you get the disease, you have two chances: one of dying, and one of not dying. And if you die—well, you still have two chances.

❧—☙

"I haven't slept for days."

"How come?"

"I only sleep at night."

❧—☙

Patient: Doctor, I have an awful pain every time I lift my arm.

Doctor: So, don't lift it.

❧—☙

Patient: My feet are always cold.

Doctor: Well, all you have to do is go to bed and have a brick at your feet.

Patient: I tried that.

Doctor: Did you get the brick hot?
Patient: Get it hot? It took me all night just to get it warm.

∽⊘—⊘∾

My arm started to hurt me and I asked the doctor to examine it. He looked at my arm and brought out a medical book and studied it for fifteen minutes. He said to me, "Have you ever had that pain before?" I said, "Yes." He said, "Well, you got it again."

ACQUAINTANCE

Jay: I understand you have a speaking acquaintance with her.
Bill: Merely a listening acquaintance.

ACTOR

Did you hear about the actor who fell off a ship as it was passing near a lighthouse? The poor fellow drowned because he persisted in swimming in circles in order to keep within the spotlight.

∽⊘—⊘∾

"A horse! A horse! My kingdom for a horse," spoke the actor dramatically from the stage.
"Would a jackass do?" called out a heckler in the balcony.
"Why yes," said the actor. "Come on down."

∽⊘—⊘∾

George: When I left the stage, the audience went wild with applause.
Harry: That's because they knew you weren't coming back!

ADAM AND EVE

Q: What is that which Adam never saw or possessed, yet left two of for each of his children?
A: Parents.

∽⊘—⊘∾

Sunday school teacher: Can anyone tell me the story of Adam and Eve?

Little girl: First God created Adam. Then He looked at him and said, "I think I could do better if I tried again." So He created Eve.

❦

I found this dry leaf in this old Bible. Do you suppose it belonged to Adam and Eve?

❦

Q: How were Adam and Eve prevented from gambling?
A: Their paradise (pair-o-dice) was taken away from them.

❦

Even Adam and Eve had their problems. One day Adam got angry. "You've done it again, Eve," said Adam. "You put my shirt in the salad again."

❦

Q: What nationality were Adam and Eve?
A: Soviet citizens, of course . . . nothing to wear, only an apple to eat, but living in paradise.

❦

Adam and Eve had many advantages, but the principal one was that they escaped teething.

❦

The only things Adam would recognize if he came back to earth are the jokes.

❦

Adam was rejected for Eden the apple.

❦

What a good thing Adam had. When he said something, he knew nobody had said it before.

∽⊖—⊝∾

Adam may have had his troubles, but at least he didn't have to listen to Eve talking about the man she could have married.

∽⊖—⊝∾

The first Adam-splitting gave us Eve, a force which ingenious men in all ages have never gotten under control.

∽⊖—⊝∾

Eve was nigh Adam; Adam was naive.

∽⊖—⊝∾

Eve: Adam, do you love me?
Adam: Who else?

∽⊖—⊝∾

Conversation between Adam and Eve must have been difficult at times because they had nobody to talk about.

∽⊖—⊝∾

Adam and Eve were the first bookkeepers; they invented the loose-leaf system.

∽⊖—⊝∾

Adam and Eve lived thousands of years B.C.—before clothing.

∽⊖—⊝∾

And here are Adam and Eve living together in paradise. You can tell it's paradise. Not once does Eve ask Adam to take out the garbage.

❦

You remember Eve, the first woman who ever said, "I haven't got a thing to wear" and meant it!

❦

Whatever other problems poor Adam may have faced, he at least never had to listen to Eve complain about other women having finer clothes than she.

❦

When Eve tried to get out of the garden without him, Adam called up to the Commanding Officer, "Eve is absent without leaf!"

❦

The Bible begins with a man and a woman in a garden and it ends with the Revelation.
—*Oscar Wilde*

ADOLESCENCE

The period in which the young suddenly feel a great responsibility about answering the telephone.

❦

A teenager who acts like a baby when you don't treat him like an adult.

AGE

"Did you see how pleased Mrs. Smith looked when I told her she didn't look a day older than her daughter?"

"I didn't notice Mrs. Smith . . . I was too busy watching the expression on her daughter's face!"

❧ — ❧

In a hat shop a saleslady gushed: "That's the hat for you. It makes you look ten years younger."

"Then I don't want it," retorted the customer. "I certainly can't afford to put on ten years every time I take off my hat!"

❧ — ❧

"I'm approaching the age of thirty."

"From which direction?"

❧ — ❧

When a woman tells you her age, it's all right to look surprised, but don't scowl.

❧ — ❧

Husband: Dear, do you remember John Williams? I saw him today. He was the student body president at our high school.

Wife: That was thirty-five years ago.

Husband: I know. In fact, he has gotten so bald and so fat he didn't even recognize me.

❧ — ❧

After a serious operation a lady was still in a coma. Her worried husband stood at the foot of her bed.

"Well," said the nurse reassuringly, "at least her age is on her side."

"She's not so young," said the husband. "She's forty-five."

At this point the patient moved slightly, and quietly but firmly murmured, "Forty-four."

AGNOSTIC

A person who says that he knows nothing about God, and when you agree with him, he becomes angry.

∽⊖—⊖∽

Agnostic is Latin for ignoramus.

∽⊖—⊖∽

Agnostic: If those Christians would stop building such large and fancy buildings and give the money to the poor, it would be more to their credit.
Christian: I've heard that remark before.
Agnostic: Indeed! And by whom, may I ask?
Christian: Judas Iscariot.

AIR-CONDITIONED

Why is it that a businessman will go from his air-conditioned house to his air-conditioned office in his air-conditioned car, then go to a health club and pay fifty dollars an hour to sweat?

∽⊖—⊖∽

"Our church should be air-conditioned," snapped Mrs. Smith. "It is unhealthy for people to sleep in a stuffy room."

AIRLINES

A good-sized man approached the airline ticket counter and asked for a reservation from Los Angeles to New York. The clerk knew that the plane was very full with baggage and passengers.

"How much do you weigh, sir?" asked the clerk.

"With or without clothes?" the passenger asked.

"Well," said the clerk, "how do you intend to travel?"

❧ ❦ ❧

Airline passenger to stewardess: I know this is the economy section, but showing the copilot's home movies is carrying it a bit too far.

❧ ❦ ❧

My airplane flight was so rough that the stewardesses poured the food directly into the sick sacks!

❧ ❦ ❧

He: Excuse me, stewardess. How high is this plane?

She: About 30,000 feet.

He: Oh, and how wide is it?

❧ ❦ ❧

The other day one of those jumbo jets took off from New York with four hundred passengers and then had to make a forced landing in Newark because of a hernia.

Alarm

An alarm clock is a small device used to wake up people who have no children.

Amateurs

I have always been confused when I hear the phrase, "professional women"—are there any amateurs?

Amen

Little Billy knelt before his bed and prayed, "Dear God, if You can find some way to put the vitamins in candy and ice cream instead of in spinach and cod liver oil, I would sure appreciate it. Amen."

❧⟶❧

We've been letting our six-year-old go to sleep listening to the radio, and I'm beginning to wonder if it's a good idea. Last night he said his prayers and wound up with, "And God bless Mommy and Daddy and Sister. Amen—and FM!"

❧⟶❧

The sermon went on and on and on in the heat of the church. At last the minister paused and asked, "What more, my friends, can I say?"
In the back of the church a voice offered earnestly, "Amen!"

American

Immigration men are knowledgeable. They are pretty clever guys. This one fellow in particular has a little trick.
He asks: "What's your nationality?"
"American."
"American, huh? Do you know the words of 'The Star Spangled Banner'?"
"No, I don't."
"You're an American; go in."

Ancestors

"My folks came over on the Mayflower."
"Don't feel bad about it. We can't all be born here."

Angel

Melba: The King of England struck one of my ancestors on the shoulder with the tip of his sword and made him a knight.

Pam: That's nothing! My grandfather was walking next to a new building when one of the carpenters dropped his hammer. It struck my grandfather on the head and made him an angel.

❦

Did you hear about the dead angel? He died of harp failure.

Anger

In our marriage we made a decision to never go to bed mad. We haven't had any sleep for three weeks.

❦

Angry wife to husband: You can't even play a friendly little game of Rook . . . no, you always have to try to win.

❦

A young girl who was writing a paper for school came to her father and asked, "Dad, what is the difference between anger and exasperation?"

The father replied, "It is mostly a matter of degree. Let me show you what I mean." With that the father went to the telephone and dialed a number at random. To the man who answered the phone, he said, "Hello, is Melvin there?" The man answered, "There is no one living here named Melvin. Why don't you learn to look up numbers before you dial them?"

"See," said the father to his daughter. "That man was not a bit happy with our call. He was probably very busy with something and we annoyed him. Now watch . . ." The father dialed the number again. "Hello, is Melvin there?" asked the father.

"Now look here!" came the heated reply. "You just called this number and I told you that there is no Melvin here! You've got a lot of nerve calling again!" The receiver slammed down hard.

The father turned to his daughter and said, "You see that was anger. Now I'll show you what exasperation means." He again dialed the same number, and when a violent voice roared, "Hello!" the father calmly said, "Hello, this is Melvin. Have there been any calls for me?"

ANIMALS

Lady: I would like a pair of alligator shoes.
Man: Yes, ma'am; what size is your alligator?

꿍—ꚳ

Did you hear the story about the fisherman who was fishing with the only thing the fish would bite on—frogs? In searching for frogs, which were rather scarce, he saw a big garden snake with a frog in its mouth, but the snake would not release it. He did not know what to do. As he looked around, he noticed an old whiskey bottle on the shore that someone had tossed aside and it still had some whiskey in it. He grabbed the bottle and poured the leftover whiskey on the snake's head. The snake finally coughed up the frog.

The fisherman baited his hook with the frog and went back to fishing. Everything was going well until he felt something crawling up his pant leg. He looked down and there was the same snake with another frog in its mouth.

꿍—ꚳ

A gorilla walked into a drugstore and ordered a fifty-cent sundae. He put down a ten-dollar bill to pay for it. The clerk thought, "What can a gorilla know about money?" So he handed back a single dollar in change.

As he did, he said, "You know, we don't get many gorillas in here."

"No wonder," answered the gorilla, "at nine dollars a sundae."

꿍—ꚳ

A man's car stopped dead as he was driving along an old country road. He got out of his car, lifted the hood, and looked at the motor. Just then, a big black and white cow came along and stopped beside him. The cow also looked under the hood at the motor.

"Your trouble is probably the carburetor," said the cow.

The startled man jumped back and ran down the road until he met a farmer. He told the farmer what had happened.

The farmer asked, "Was the cow black and white?"

"Yes, yes!" cried the motorist.

"Oh, don't pay attention to Old Bossy. She doesn't know a thing about cars."

Answer Man

Q: What do you get if you cross a chicken with an elephant?
A: I don't know, but Colonel Sanders would have a lot of trouble trying to dip it into the batter.

❦

Q: If a man dies in England who was born in China, reared in France, worked in South America, and married in Japan, what is he?
A: Dead.

❦

Q: Why did Humpty Dumpty have a great fall?
A: To make up for a terrible summer.

❦

Q: A man who always remembers a woman's birthday but forgets her age is called what?
A: A smart man.

❦

Q: What is the best way to keep fish from smelling?
A: Cut off their noses.

❦

Q: What do you call a funeral where you smell your own flowers?
A: A wedding.

Q: What is the difference between the North Pole and the South Pole?
A: All the difference in the world.

Q: If a man crosses the ocean twice without taking a bath, what is he called?
A: A dirty double-crosser.

Q: What do you get when you cross an elephant with a computer?
A: A 5,000 pound know-it-all!

Q: What is the difference between unlawful and illegal?
A: Illegal is a sick bird.

ANTIQUES

Being an antique dealer is a strange way to make a living. It's the only business where the grandparents buy something, the parents sell it, and the grandchildren buy it again.

APATHY

The number-one problem in our country is apathy—but who cares!

Aptitude Tests

An executive came home and slumped in his favorite chair with a discouraged look. His wife asked what was wrong.

"You know these aptitude tests we're giving at the office? Well, I took one today for fun. It's a good thing I own the company!"

Argument

If you really want the last word in an argument, try saying, "I guess you're right."

Armageddon

Ad in newspaper:
ARMAGEDDON—THE EARTH'S LAST WAR—HOW AND WHERE IT WILL BE FOUGHT—At the First Baptist Church

Army

During an Army war game a commanding officer's jeep got stuck in the road. The C.O. saw some men lounging nearby and asked them to help him get unstuck.

"Sorry, sir," said one of the loafers, "but we've been classified dead and the umpire said we couldn't contribute in any way."

The C.O. turned to his driver and said, "Go drag a couple of those dead bodies over here and throw them under the wheels to give us some traction."

∽⌒∾

Officer: Soldier, do you have change for a dollar?
Soldier: Sure, buddy.

Officer: That's no way to address an officer. Now, let's try that again. Soldier, do you have change for a dollar?

Soldier: No, sir!

❦

The first sergeant was holding a class on combat for his company. He said, "LaHaye, what would you do if you saw seven hundred enemy soldiers coming at you?"

LaHaye said, "I would shoot them all with my rifle."

The sergeant asked, "On the right you see four hundred enemy soldiers charging at you. What would you do?"

LaHaye said, "I would shoot them with my rifle."

The sergeant continued, "Okay! On your left, LaHaye, you notice one thousand enemy soldiers heading straight at you. What would you do?"

LaHaye answered again, "I would shoot them all with my rifle."

The sergeant yelled, "Just a minute, LaHaye. Where are you getting all those bullets?"

The soldier smiled and said, "The same place you're getting all those enemy soldiers."

❦

The new Army recruit was given guard duty at 2 A.M. He did his best for awhile, but about 4 A.M. he went to sleep. He awakened to find the officer of the day standing before him.

Remembering the heavy penalty for being asleep on guard duty, this smart young man kept his head bowed for another moment, then looked upward and reverently said, "A-a-amen!"

ARTIST

"I heard about an artist who painted a cobweb on the ceiling so realistically that the maid spent hours trying to get it down."

"Sorry, I don't believe it."

"Why not? Artists have been known to do such things."

"Yes, but maids haven't."

❦

Model: The light's too strong. This chair is too hard. I can't stand this dress. My hair's a mess. My lipstick is the wrong color.
Artist: What is your name?
Model: Lisa.
So the painter called the work "The Moaner Lisa."

ATHEISM

Nobody talks so constantly about God as those who insist that there is no God.

❦

An atheist is one point beyond the devil.

❦

Some are atheists only in fair weather.

❦

By night an atheist half believes in God.

❦

How to wipe out an atheist: Serve him a meal and then ask him if he believes there is a cook.

❦

Atheist: Do you honestly believe that Jonah spent three days and nights in the belly of a whale?
Preacher: I don't know, sir, but when I get to heaven I'll ask him.
Atheist: But suppose he isn't in heaven?
Preacher: Then you ask him!

❦

One day a little girl was visiting Sunday school when her teacher asked her to which denomination her relatives belonged. "Is it Baptists, Lutherans, Presbyterians, Seventh-day Adventists, or Methodists?" asked the teacher.

The little girl replied, "I think they are six-day atheists."

❦

An atheist is one who hopes the Lord will do nothing to disturb his disbelief.
—*Franklin P. Jones*

❦

The chief fault with atheism is that it has no support.

❦

Did you hear about the son of the atheists who asked his parents: "Do you think God knows we don't believe in Him?"

AUSTRALIA

An American was knocked unconscious in a traffic accident in Australia. The ambulance took him to a local hospital. When he finally woke up he asked the nurse, "Was I brought here to die?"

"No," said the nurse, "you were brought in here yesterdye."

⊰ B ⊱

BABY

An alimentary canal with a loud voice at one end and no responsibility at the other.

⌾—⌾

Getting the baby to sleep is the hardest when she is about eighteen years old.

⌾—⌾

Husband: It must be time to get up.
Wife: How can you tell?
Husband: The baby has fallen asleep at last.

⌾—⌾

Mother: The baby is the image of his father.
Neighbor: What do you care, so long as he is healthy?

⌾—⌾

The phone rang in the maternity ward and an excited voice on the other end said: "This is George Smith and I'm bringing my wife in . . . she's about to have a baby!"
"Calm down," replied the attendant. "Tell me, is this her first baby?"
"No," the voice replied, "this is her husband."

⌾—⌾

For weeks a six-year-old lad kept telling his first-grade teacher about the baby brother or sister that was expected at his house. One day the mother allowed the boy to feel the movements of the unborn child. The six-year-old was obviously impressed, but made no comment. Furthermore, he stopped telling his teacher about the impending event. The

21

teacher finally sat the boy on her lap and said, "Tommy, whatever has become of that baby brother or sister you were expecting at home?"

Tommy burst into tears and confessed, "I think Mommy ate it!"

BACKSEAT DRIVER

Wife: This traffic jam is terrible. What shall I do?

Husband: I don't know, but I'm sure if you climb into the backseat you can figure it out.

⚮—⚮

Bud: All this talk about backseat driving is hogwash. I've driven for fifteen years and I've never heard a word from back there.

Dud: What kind of car do you drive?

Bud: A hearse.

⚮—⚮

"Daddy, before you married Mommy, who told you how to drive?"

BAD DRIVER

Did you hear about the cheerful truck driver who pulled up at a road-side cafe in the middle of the night for a dinner stop? Halfway through his dinner, three wild-looking motorcyclists roared up . . . bearded, leather-jacketed, filthy . . . with swastikas adorning their chests and helmets.

For no reason at all, they selected the truck driver as a target. One poured pepper over his head, another stole his apple pie, the third deliberately upset his cup of coffee. The truck driver never said one word—just arose, paid his check, and exited.

"That truck driver sure ain't much of a fighter," sneered one of the invaders. The girl behind the counter, peering out into the night, added, "He doesn't seem to be much of a driver either. He just ran his truck right over three motorcycles."

⚮—⚮

Boy: Dad, Mom just backed the car out of the garage and ran over my bicycle.
Father: Serves you right, Son, for leaving it on the front lawn.

***

Nothing is more exasperating than getting in the lane behind a guy who is observing the speed limit.

BAD SITUATION

Talk about bad situations . . . just think about
* a screen door on a submarine
* a stowaway on a kamikaze plane
* a teenager who parks in a dark alley with his girl and his horn gets stuck
* a soup sandwich
* one who ejects from a helicopter
* a Hindu snake charmer with a deaf cobra

BALD

Ken: I find that split hair is a problem.
Bob: Yeah, you're right. Mine split about five years ago.

***

What a wife said about her baldheaded husband: I love to run my fingers through his hair because I can make better time on the open road.

***

If a man is bald in front, he's a thinker. If he's bald in the back, he's a lover. If he's bald in front and back, he thinks he's a lover.

***

He's so bald he walks into a barber shop and asks for a shave and a shave.

∾⊝——⊝∽

He is so bald that it looks like his neck is blowing a bubble.

∾⊝——⊝∽

He has wavy hair . . . it's waving good-bye.

∾⊝——⊝∽

Melba: I notice by this article that men become bald much more than women because of the intense activity of their brains.

Ken: Yes, and I notice that women don't grow beards because of the intense activity of their chins!

∾⊝——⊝∽

"Papa, are you growing taller all the time?"
"No, my child. Why do you ask?"
"'Cause the top of your head is poking up through your hair."

∾⊝——⊝∽

"There's a new remedy on the market for baldness. It's made of alum and persimmon juice. It doesn't grow hair, but it shrinks your head to fit what hair you have."

BAPTISM

A Methodist and a Baptist were arguing the virtues of their baptisms. The Methodist said, "All right, if I take a man and lead him in the water to his ankles, is he baptized?"

"No," said the Baptist.

"Till just the top of his head is showing above the water, is he baptized?"

"No."

"All right, then," asserted the Methodist. "That's where we baptize them."

⤸—⤷

A Presbyterian minister was about to baptize a baby. Turning to the father, he inquired, "His name, please?"

"William Patrick Arthur Timothy John MacArthur."

The minister turned to his assistant and said, "A little more water, please."

⤸—⤷

I don't mind going to a church service in a drive-in theater. But when they hold the baptisms in a car wash, that's going too far!

BAPTIST

Q: When you have fifty people, all of different opinions, what do you have?

A: A Baptist church.

⤸—⤷

"Baptist fellowship is heavenly."

"Yeah, heaven is the only place it will work."

⤸—⤷

Several churches in the South decided to hold union services. The leader was a Baptist and proud of his denomination.

"How many Baptists are here?" he asked on the first night of the revival.

All except one little old lady raised their hands.

"Lady, what are you?" asked the leader.

"I'm a Methodist," meekly replied the lady.

"Why are you a Methodist?" queried the leader.

"Well," replied the little old lady, "my grandparents were Methodists, my mother was a Methodist, and my late husband was a Methodist."

"Well," retorted the leader, "just supposing all your relatives had been morons, what would that have made you?"

"Oh, I see. A Baptist, I suppose," the lady replied meekly.

BARBER

A brilliant conversationalist, who occasionally shaves and cuts hair.

❦

Barber to a customer with a lot of grease on his hair: Do you want it cut or just an oil change?

❦

Customer: Before you begin, I want you to know that I like the weather that we are having, I have no interest in baseball or football, I do not want to hear who won the prize fights, I am not interested in the latest newspaper scandals, and I don't want to discuss political issues. Now, go ahead with your work.

Barber: Okay. And if it won't offend you, sir, I will be able to do my work better and faster if you don't talk so much.

❦

A man entered a barber shop and asked for a shave. After the shave, the barber said, "That will be ten cents, please."

"But," said the man, "your sign says $1.25 for a shave. How come only ten cents?"

The barber answered, "Once in awhile we get a guy that is all mouth and we only charge him a dime!"

❦

I couldn't stand my boy's long hair any longer, so I dragged him to the barber shop with me and ordered, "Give him a crew cut." The barber did just that, and so help me, I found I'd been bringing up somebody else's son!

BASEBALL

Baseball is talked about a great deal in the Bible: . . . In the big inning . . . Eve stole first . . . Adam stole second . . . Gideon rattled the pitchers . . . Goliath was put out by David . . . Prodigal Son made a home run . . .

❧

Although (*insert name of baseball player*) was not a good fielder, he was not a good hitter, either.

❧

One young woman at her first baseball game said that she liked the pitcher the best "because he hit the bat every time."

BEAUTY

"And when I was sixteen, the president of the United States presented me with a beauty award."
"Really? I didn't think Lincoln bothered with that sort of thing!"

BEHAVIOR

The reason the way of the transgressor is hard is because it's so crowded.

BIBLE

Most people are bothered by those passages of Scripture they do not understand, but the passages that bother me are those I do understand.
—*Mark Twain*

❧

The Bible must be the Word of God to withstand such poor preaching through the years.

Bible Quiz

Q: When were automobiles first mentioned in the Bible?
A: When Elijah went up high.

❧ ——— ❧

Q: What simple affliction brought about the death of Samson?
A: Fallen arches.

❧ ——— ❧

Q: Who was the most successful physician in the Bible?
A: Job; he had the most patience (patients).

❧ ——— ❧

Q: Who was the best financier in the Bible?
A: Noah; he floated his stock while the whole world was in liquidation.

❧ ——— ❧

Q: Who was the straightest man in the Bible?
A: Joseph. Pharoah made a ruler out of him.

Big Men

"Have any big men ever been born in this town?"
"No, just little babies."

Bigamy

The extreme penalty for bigamy is two mothers-in-law.

BILL

Virginia: When was your son born?
Beverly: In March. He came on the first of the month.
Virginia: Is that why you call him Bill?

❦

Wife: There is a man at the door who wants to see you about a bill you owe him. He wouldn't give his name.
Husband: What does he look like?
Wife: He looks like you had better pay him.

BIRDS

"A little bird told me."
"It must have been a stool pigeon."

❦

A Californian was visiting his Texan cousin and while walking with the cousin across a barren section of land, saw a funny-looking bird flop across the road in front of them. "What is it?" the Californian asked.
"It's a bird of paradise," replied his Texan cousin.
The Californian replied, "Long way from home, isn't he?"

BIRTH CONTROL

"Do you know what the best birth control method in the world is?"
"No."
"That's it."

BIRTHDAY

Husband to wife: How do you expect me to remember your birthday when you never look any older?

❦

Do not put any candles on my birthday cake—I don't want to make light of my age.

❦

Today is the fifth anniversary of my wife's thirty-ninth birthday.

BITTER

"I have a bitter taste in my mouth."
"Been biting your tongue?"

BLABBERMOUTH

Postlude—To guests he is the gracious host,
To children three he is "the most,"
To loving wife the perfect mate,
To fellow workers he's "just great!"
How *sad* then that a humble friend
Upon his promise can't depend,
From east to west, from north to south
His name? You guessed it! *Blabbermouth!*

BLUNDER

Mark Twain was once asked the difference between a mistake and blunder. He explained it this way: "If you walk into a restaurant and walk out with someone's silk umbrella and leave your own cotton one, that is a mistake. But if you pick up someone's cotton umbrella and leave your own silk one, that is a blunder."

BOOB TUBE

Joe: Did you know there are 60 million TV sets in our country and only 45 million bathtubs?
Moe: No, I didn't, but what does that prove?
Joe: Just that there are 15 million dirty people watching TV.

❦

When an old TV star's show was canceled by the powers that be, a fan asked him, "Do you answer personally the hundreds of letters that come in every day demanding that your program be renewed?" He answered disarmingly, "Goodness, no! I scarcely have time to write them!"

∽⊙——⊙∽

Nowadays a good conversationalist is anyone who can talk louder than the hi-fi or TV.

THE BOOK OF PARABLES

Recently I interviewed a _____ (teacher, student, or whoever) from _____ (name of church, school, or organization you are speaking to) and asked (him/her) some Bible questions. I could tell that they had really learned a great deal, so I asked them what their favorite book of the Bible was. They said, "The New Testament." I replied, "What part of the New Testament?" They said, "Oh, by far, I love the Book of Parables best." I asked, "Would you kindly relate one of those parables to me?"

They said, "Once upon a time, a man went from Jerusalem to Jericho and fell among thieves. The thieves threw him into the weeds, and the weeds grew up and choked that man. He then went on and met the Queen of Sheba and she gave that man a thousand talents of gold and silver and a hundred changes of raiment. He then got in his chariot and drove furiously to the Red Sea. When he got there, the waters parted and he drove to the other side.

"On the other side he drove under a big olive tree and got his hair caught on a limb and was left hanging there. He hung there many days and many nights and the ravens brought him food to eat and water to drink. One night while he was hanging there asleep his wife Delilah came along and cut off his hair, and he dropped and fell on stony ground. The children of a nearby city came out and said, 'Go up, thou baldhead, go up, thou baldhead.' And the man cursed the children and two she-bears came out of the woods and tore up the children.

"Then it began to rain and it rained for forty days and forty nights. And he went and hid himself in a cave. Later he went out and met a man and said, 'Come and take supper with me.' But the man replied, 'I cannot come for I have married a wife.' So he went out into the highways and byways and compelled them to come in, but they would not heed his call.

"He then went on to Jericho and blew his trumpet seven times and the city walls came tumbling down. As he walked by one of the damaged buildings in the city, he saw Queen Jezebel sitting high up in a window and when she saw him she laughed and made fun of him. The man grew furious and said, 'Toss her down.' And they did. Then he said, 'Toss her down again.' And they did. They threw her down seventy times seven. And the fragments they gathered up were twelve baskets full. The question now is . . . 'Whose wife will she be on the day of resurrection?'"

Books

"I'm really worried."
"Why?"
"Well, my wife read *A Tale of Two Cities* and we had twins. Later she read *The Three Musketeers* and we had triplets. Now she is reading *Birth of a Nation!*"

❦

A collector of rare books ran into an acquaintance of his who had just thrown away an old Bible that had been in his family for generations. He happened to mention that Guten something had printed it.

"Not Gutenberg?" gasped the book collector.

"Yes, that was the name."

"You idiot! You've thrown away one of the first books ever printed. A copy recently sold at an auction for $400,000."

"Mine wouldn't have been worth a dime," replied the man. "Some clown by the name of Martin Luther had scribbled all over it."

❦

If you think no evil, see no evil, and hear no evil, the chances are that you'll never write a bestselling novel.

BORE

A person who has nothing to say and says it.

✺

One who opens his mouth and puts his feats in.

✺

A tired minister was at home resting. But through the window he saw a woman approaching his door. She was one of those too-talkative people and he was not anxious to talk with her. He said to his wife, "I'll just duck upstairs and wait until she goes away."

An hour passed. He tiptoed to the stair landing and listened. Not a sound. He was very pleased so he started down calling loudly to his wife, "Well, my dear, did you get rid of that old bore at last?"

The next moment he heard the voice of the same woman caller, and she couldn't possibly have missed hearing him. Two steps down, he saw them both staring up at him. It seemed truly a crisis moment.

The quick-thinking minister's wife answered, "Yes, dear, she went away over an hour ago. But Mrs. Jones has come to call in the meantime and I'm sure you'll be glad to greet her."

BOSS

The one who is early when you are late and late when you are early.

✺

The thing mother allows father to think that he is.

BOWLING

Did you hear the one about the ministers who formed a bowling team? Called themselves the Holy Rollers.

Boy Meets Father

"Young man," said the angry father from the head of the stairs, "didn't I hear the clock strike four when you brought my daughter in?"

"You did," admitted the boyfriend. "It was going to strike eleven, but I grabbed it and held the gong so it wouldn't disturb you."

The father muttered, "Doggone! Why didn't I think of that one in my courting days!"

∽—∾

She: You finally asked Daddy for my hand in marriage. What did he say?

He: Not a word. He just fell on my neck and sobbed.

Boy Meets Girl

One girl to another: There's never a dull moment when you're out with Wilbur—it lasts the whole evening.

∽—∾

On a lonely, moonlit country road as the car engine coughed and the car came to a halt, the following conversation took place:

"That's funny," said the young man. "I wonder what that knocking was?"

"Well, I can tell you one thing for sure," the girl answered icily. "It wasn't opportunity."

∽—∾

A modest girl never pursues a man, nor does a mousetrap pursue a mouse.

∽—∾

Boy to girl: Filet mignon? It's pickled goat's liver. Why?

∽—∾

One of the unmarried girls who works in a busy office arrived early the other morning and began passing out cigars and candy, both tied with blue ribbons. When asked what the occasion was, she proudly displayed a diamond solitaire on her third finger, left hand, and announced, "It's a boy . . . six feet tall and 187 pounds."

—⊙—⊙—

Boy: I'm afraid we'll have to stop here; the engine's getting pretty warm.
Girl: You men are such hypocrites; you always say the engine.

—⊙—⊙—

She: You remind me of Don Juan.
He (flattered): Tell me just how.
She: Well, for one thing, he's been dead for years.

—⊙—⊙—

Girl: You remind me of an ocean.
Boy: You mean wild . . . restless . . . and romantic?
Girl: No, you just make me sick.

—⊙—⊙—

He: If you would give me your phone number I would give you a call.
She: It's in the book.
He: Good, what is your name?
She: It's in the book, too.

—⊙—⊙—

After a Dutch-treat-on-everything date, the girl responded to her escort who brought her home, "Since we've gone Dutch on everything else, you can just kiss yourself goodnight!"

—⊙—⊙—

Girl: Would you like to take a walk?
Boy: I'd love to.
Girl: Well, don't let me detain you.

⌖

Conceited: I can tell just by looking into a girl's eyes exactly how she feels about me.
Girl: Gee, that must be embarrassing for you.

⌖

Boy: You look prettier every minute. Do you know what that is a sign of?
Girl: Yes, you are about to run out of gas.

⌖

Girl: The man I marry must be brave as a lion, but not forward; handsome as Apollo, but not conceited; wise as Solomon, but meek as a lamb; a man who is kind to every woman, but loves only me.
Boy: How lucky we met.

⌖

"Without you, everything is dark and dreary . . . the clouds gather and the wind beats the rain . . . then comes the warm sun . . . you are like a rainbow."
"Is this a proposal or a weather report?"

⌖

Boy: If you refuse to be mine, I'll hurl myself off that 500–foot cliff over there.
Girl: That's a lot of bluff.

⌖

Boy: Please whisper those three little words that will make me walk on air.

Girl: Go hang yourself.

⌒⊖—⊝⌒

Boy: What would I have to give you for one little kiss?
Girl: Chloroform!

⌒⊖—⊝⌒

Boy: Why don't you marry me? Is there someone else?
Girl: There must be.

⌒⊖—⊝⌒

Bill: Am I the only man you ever have kissed?
Sue: Yes, and by far the best-looking.

⌒⊖—⊝⌒

Dave: My girlfriend's really smart. She has brains enough for two.
Jeff: Sounds like the right girl for you.

⌒⊖—⊝⌒

One of Joe's bunkmates broke up with his girlfriend. The girlfriend wrote demanding that he return her photograph immediately. The soldier borrowed a collection of several pictures of various girls and sent them to his ex-sweetheart with her photo tucked in among them. He enclosed a note:

"Dear Mildred, pick out yours. I have forgotten what you look like."

⌒⊖—⊝⌒

Boy: Will you marry me?
Girl: No, but I'll always admire your good taste.

⌒⊖—⊝⌒

Man: Pardon me, young lady, but in the matter of dress, don't you think you could show a little more discretion?

Girl: My gosh, some of you guys are never satisfied.

⚬⊖⚬

PK: She said I'm interesting, brave, and intelligent.

Bob: You should never go steady with a girl who deceives you from the very start.

⚬⊖⚬

Joe: I was selected by a computer as an ideal boyfriend.

Moe: Who wants to be a computer's boyfriend?

⚬⊖⚬

Joe: What's so unusual about your girlfriend?

Moe: She chews on her nails.

Joe: Lots of girls chew on their nails.

Moe: Toenails?

⚬⊖⚬

He: I promise you, the next time you contradict me, I'm going to kiss you.

She: Oh no you're not!

BRAINS

"How long can a man live without brains?"
"I don't know. How old are you?"

⚬⊖⚬

"Be quiet. You're interrupting my train of thought."
"Let me know when it comes to a station."

⚬⊖⚬

He spends half his time trying to be witty. You might say he's a half-wit.

❦

He has a small birthmark on his head . . . his brain.

❦

Have you ever considered No-Cal shampoo? It's especially made for fatheads.

❦

You really have an open mind . . . and a mouth to match.

❦

"I've got an idea."
"Be kind to it. It's a long way from home."

❦

Blow: Did you hear the smartest kid in the world is becoming deaf?
Joe: No, tell me about it.
Blow: What did you say?

❦

Why don't you pal around with a half-wit so you can have someone to look up to!

❦

Two men drove their cars toward each other on a narrow street—neither could pass. One leaned out and shouted, "I never back up for a stupid idiot!"
"I always do!" shouted the other man, shifting into reverse.

❦

Melba: I can't decide whether to go to a palmist or to a mind reader.
Ken: Go to a palmist. It's obvious that you have a palm.

⚮

Bill: I've got a splinter in my finger.
Jill: How did you get it . . . scratch your head?

⚮

Let's play horse. I'll be the front end . . . you just be yourself.

BRAT

A child who acts like your own but belongs to someone else.

BREATH

"Oh, I can't catch my breath."
"With your breath you should be thankful."

⚮

Husband: This report says that every time I breathe, three Chinese die!
Wife: That doesn't surprise me! You've got to stop eating so much garlic.

BULLETIN BOARD

In front of church: "You are not too bad to come in. You are not too good to stay out."

BURGLARS

George: My dad's very rich, so I don't know what to give him for Christmas. What do you give to a man who has everything?
Harold: A burglar alarm.

⚮

The other day a guy pointed a gun at me and said, "Stick 'em up and congratulations!" I said, "What's the congratulations for?" He said, "You are now entering a lower tax bracket."

⇛—⇚

The robber stuck a gun in the man's back, but the man turned suddenly, applied a judo grip, and flung the robber across the alley. Then he pounced on the robber and began to wipe him out. He blackened his eyes, broke his jaw, fractured his ribs, and broke both his arms. Finally the crook cried in desperation, "Hey Mister, ain't you never gonna call a cop?"

⇛—⇚

A burglar entered the house of a Quaker and proceeded to rob it. The Quaker heard noises and took his shotgun downstairs and found the burglar. He aimed his gun and said gently: "Friend, I mean thee no harm, but thou standest where I am about to shoot."

BURNT OFFERINGS

Teacher: In our lesson today we have talked about the burnt offerings offered in the Old Testament. Why don't we have burnt offerings today?

Student: On account of air pollution.

BUS

There's a bus leaving in ten minutes. Be under it!

⇛—⇚

The bus was very crowded . . . the highway was very busy . . . and the road was snow-covered. A woman passenger persisted in asking the driver if he had come to her stop yet.

Finally she asked, "How will I know when we get to my stop?"

The driver said, "By the big smile on my face, lady."

⇛—⇚

"Are you enjoying the bus ride?"
"Yes!"
"Then why are you riding with your eyes shut? Are you sick?"
"No, I'm okay. It's just that I hate to see women stand."

BUSINESS

Art: How's business?
Ted: Terrible. Even the people who never pay have stopped buying.

≈—≈

Business was pretty bad at Max's Bargain Emporium. Then, to compound his troubles, Harry's on his right decided to run a big Going-Out-Of-Business Sale and hung up a sign reading: THE GREATEST GOING-OUT-OF-BUSINESS SALE EVER. YOU COULDN'T GET BIGGER BARGAINS IF WE WERE REALLY GOING OUT OF BUSINESS.

Then Leo, on Max's left, decided to run a sale and hung up a sign reading: FIRE SALE. YOU COULDN'T GET BETTER BUYS EVEN IF THERE WAS A REAL FIRE.

Max joined the fun. He hung up a sign directly between the others reading: ENTRANCE TO SALE.

≈—≈

The chief executive of a large corporation, who was a stickler for efficiency, made an inspection tour of one of the company's manufacturing units. As he led his subordinates from department to department, he was proud as a peacock as the machines hummed and the men worked swiftly and efficiently.

Suddenly the executive heard some whistling from behind a stack of boxes. He confronted the whistler, who was lying down on some of the boxes.

"What is your salary?" demanded the chief executive.

"Who me?" said the whistler.

"Yes, you."

"I make $100 a week," replied the young man as he continued whistling.

The chief executive was furious. He turned to one of his aides and said, "Give this young man $100 and get him out of here at once."

One of the courageous assistants said, "But C.J., he . . ."

"You heard me, $100 and move him out now."

Later that day the accounting department called the chief executive about the whistler.

"What account should we charge the $100 to, C.J.?"

"Payroll, naturally," said the executive in a huff.

"But C.J., that boy didn't work for us. He was a messenger waiting for a delivery receipt."

Busy

No matter how busy people are, they are never too busy to stop and talk about how busy they are.

Butcher

The customer wanted to buy a chicken and the butcher had only one in stock. He weighed it and said, "A beauty. That will be $1.25, lady."

"Oh, that's not quite large enough," said the customer. The butcher put the chicken back in the refrigerator, rolled it around on the ice several times, then put it back on the scales again.

"This one is $1.85," he said, adding his thumb for good weight.

"Oh, that's fine!" said the customer. "I'll take both of them."

❧ ☙

Customer: Look, you are giving me a big piece of bone. With meat as expensive as it is, I don't want all that bone.

Butcher: I'm not giving it to you, lady, you're paying for it.

❧ C ❧

C.P.N.

Myrlene: He's a C.P.N.
Sharon: You mean C.P.A.: Certified Public Accountant.
Myrlene: No, C.P.N. Constant Pain in the Neck.

CAIN

Heckler: Who was Cain's wife?
Preacher: I respect any seeker of knowledge, but I want to warn you, young man, don't risk being lost to salvation by too much inquiring after other men's wives.

CAMP LETTERS

Dear Mom and Dad,
    Camp is okay, I think. We went hiking yesterday. Send my other tennis shoe if you can.
    Love,
    Robbie

❧—❧

Dear Mom and Dad,
    The camp director is making everyone write home.
    Tammy
    Camp Itchagooy
    Hideaway Village, Washington

❧—❧

Dear Mr. and Mrs. Phillips:
    Your daughter Lisa is having a terrific time at camp. Everyone on the staff thinks she is great. She is very popular with everyone in her

cabin. We just wanted you to know how much we appreciate having her at Camp Itchagooy. You can be very proud of her.

Most sincerely,
David Ferriera, Director

R.E, Phillips
2972 East Willson Ave.
Willacke, Washington

Dear Mr. Ferriera:

My wife and I were very excited and pleased to learn that Lisa was having a fun time at camp. Being popular is very important. We are most proud of Lisa.

We have a daughter at Camp Itchagooy, too. Her name is Christy. It would be very nice of you to let us know how she is doing.

Warmly yours,
R.E. Phillips, Father

CANNIBALS

A cannibal chief had captured a man near his camp and said to the man, "What is your profession?" The man replied, "I was editor of my company paper." "Good," smiled the cannibal chief. "Tomorrow you will be editor-in-chief."

❦

A resourceful missionary fell into the hands of a band of cannibals. "Going to eat me, I take it," said the missionary. "You wouldn't like me." He took out his pocketknife, sliced a piece from the calf of his leg, and handed it to the chief. "Try it and see for yourself," he urged. The chief took one bite, grunted, and spat. The missionary remained on the island fifty years. He had a cork leg.

❦

Then there's the missionary the cannibal couldn't boil. He was a friar.

CAPTAIN

A young man made a great deal of money in real estate. He decided to buy himself a small yacht. He then bought the proper clothes and decked himself out in the regalia of a captain.

His first visitor on board his new yacht was his grandmother. He took her on a tour of the boat. In the process, the grandson pointed to his cap with crossed anchors on it and said, "This signifies that I am a captain."

The grandmother made no comment.

"You don't seem very impressed," said the young man.

"If you want me to be impressed, I'll be impressed," said his grandmother. "To yourself, you're a captain. To me, you're maybe a captain. But to captains, you're no captain."

CARS

Those little cars have all kinds of advantages. Just this morning a motorcycle cop was chasing my Volkswagen. I knew I couldn't outrun him so I did the next best thing—drove up on the sidewalk and got lost in a crowd!

⟡

A man returned to his sports car to find a freshly crushed fender and this note affixed to his windshield wiper: "The people who saw me side-swipe your fender are now watching me write this note, and doubtless figure I'm telling you my name and address so you can contact me and send me the bill. Ho! Ho! Ho! You should live so long."

CAT

An elderly widower loved his cat so dearly he tried to teach it to talk. "If I can get Tabby to converse with me," he reasoned, "I won't have to bother with ornery humans at all." First, he tried a diet of canned salmon, then one of canaries. Tabby obviously approved of both but she didn't learn to talk. Then one day the widower had two parrots cooked in butter and served to Tabby with asparagus and French-fried potatoes. Tabby licked the plate clean, and then . . . wonder of wonders . . . suddenly turned to her master and shouted, "Look out!"

Possibly the widower didn't hear because he never moved a muscle. The next moment the ceiling caved in and buried him under a mass of debris. The cat shook its head and said in disgust, "Eight years he spends getting me to talk and then the idiot doesn't listen."

⚬—⚬

A bachelor kept a cat for companionship, and loved his cat more than life. He was planning a trip to England and entrusted the cat to his brother's care.

As soon as he arrived in England, he called his brother. "How is my cat?" he asked.

"Your cat is dead," came the reply.

"Oh my," he exclaimed. "Did you have to tell me that way?"

"How else can I tell you that your cat's dead?" inquired the brother.

"You should have led me up to it gradually," said the bachelor. "For example, when I called tonight you could have told me my cat was on the roof, but the Fire Department is getting it down. When I called tomorrow night, you could have told me they dropped him and broke his back, but a fine surgeon is doing all he can for him. Then, when I called the third night, you could have told me the surgeon did all he could but my cat passed away. That way it wouldn't have been such a shock.

"By the way," he continued, "how's Mother?"

"Mother?" came the reply. "Oh, she's up on the roof, but the Fire Department is getting her down."

⚬—⚬

In front of a delicatessen, an art connoisseur noticed a mangy little kitten lapping up milk from a saucer. The saucer, he realized with a start, was a rare and precious piece of pottery.

He sauntered into the store and offered two dollars for the cat. "It's not for sale," said the proprietor.

"Look," said the collector, "that cat is dirty and undesirable, but I'm eccentric. I like cats that way. I'll raise my offer to five dollars."

"It's a deal," said the proprietor, and pocketed the five on the spot.

"For that sum I'm sure you won't mind throwing in the saucer," said the connoisseur. "The kitten seems so happy drinking from it."

"Nothing doing," said the proprietor firmly. "That's my lucky saucer. From that saucer, so far this week I've sold 34 cats."

CEMETERY

Gary: Why are cemeteries in the middle of some towns?
Larry: Because they are dead centers.

CHAPLAIN

A couple was touring the Capitol in Washington and the guide pointed to a tall, benevolent gentleman as the congressional chaplain.

The lady asked, "What does the chaplain do? Does he pray for the Senate or House?"

The guide answered, "No, he gets up, looks at the Congress, then prays for the country!"

CHICKEN

Q: Which came first, the chicken or the egg?
A: The chicken, of course. God couldn't lay an egg.

∽☉—☉∼

Did you hear about the count who sold the king's crown? They tried and tried to make him confess but he would not. Finally, they said, "We will chop off your head if you don't tell us." He would not tell them so they took him to the chopping block. They told him that he would have one more chance but he did not take it. As the head chopper started down with the axe, the count said, "All right, I'll tell you." It was too late . . . his head went rolling to the ground.

Moral: Don't hatchet your counts before they chicken.

CHILDREN

"Darling," scolded the mother, "you shouldn't always keep everything for yourself. I have told you before that you should let your brother play with your toys half of the time."

"I've been doing it. I take the sled going downhill, and he takes it going up."

◦❄—❄◦

An old Chinaman was eating too much rice, especially since he was too frail to work. Because the grandfather had become a burden, the father of the home, his son, determined to get rid of him. He put him in a wheelbarrow, then started up the mountain. The little eight-year-old grandson went along. He was full of questions. His father explained that the grandfather was old and useless and the only thing they could do was to take him up to the mountain and leave him to die. Then the grandson had a bright idea. "I'm glad you brought me along, Father, because when you're old, I'll know where to take you."

CHILDREN OF ISRAEL

"Daddy, I want to ask you a question," said little Bobby after his first day in Sunday school.

"Yes, Bobby, what is it?"

"The teacher was reading the Bible to us—all about the children of Israel building the temple, the children of Israel crossing the Red Sea, the children of Israel making sacrifices. Didn't the grown-ups do anything?"

CHOP TO THE EGO

"Whatever I say goes."

"Then why don't you talk about yourself for awhile."

CHRISTMAS

I love Christmas. I receive a lot of wonderful presents I can't wait to exchange.

◦❄—❄◦

A famous writer once sent Christmas cards containing nothing but twenty-five letters of the alphabet. When some of his friends admitted that they had failed to understand his message, he pointed to the card and said, "Look! No L!"

CHURCH

I don't want to say it was a cold church, but the ushers were using ice skates.

⁓◦—◦⁓

"If absence makes the heart grow fonder," said a minister, "a lot of folks must love our church."

⁓◦—◦⁓

"Why don't you come to my church this next Sunday?"
"Because I belong to another abomination."

⁓◦—◦⁓

A member of the church came to the pastor and said, "Pastor, my six brethren are all asleep, and I alone have remained awake to worship God."
The pastor replied, "You had better been asleep yourself if your worship of God consists of accusations against your brethren."

⁓◦—◦⁓

A certain congregation was about to erect a new church edifice. The building committee, in consecutive meetings, passed the fellowship resolutions:

1. We shall build a new church.
2. The new building is to be located on the site of the old one.
3. The material in the old building is to be used in the new one.
4. We shall continue to use the old building until the new one is completed.

⁓◦—◦⁓

A church is a place where you encounter nodding acquaintances.

⌒⊝—⊝⌒

Pastor: Mrs. Smith, I really appreciate your devotion. You are present at all services.

Mrs. Smith: Yes, it is such a relief after a long, hard week of work. I just love to come to church, sit down on the soft cushions, and not think about anything for an hour.

⌒⊝—⊝⌒

A visiting pastor at a country church asked one of the farmers if he could use his barn to get away where it was quiet and study for his message. After several hours of study, the pastor left the barn for a walk. When he came back he discovered that the cow had eaten all of his sermon notes. The next day the farmer complained to the pastor that this cow had gone dry.

⌒⊝—⊝⌒

Deacon Johnson seemed to always fall asleep during the sermon on Sunday morning. His wife grew very tired of his behavior and she decided to deal with the embarrassing situation. The next Sunday when her husband fell asleep, she quietly removed some Limburger cheese from her purse and carefully passed it beneath his nose. Whereupon Deacon Johnson was heard to murmur, "No, Helen, no—don't kiss me now."

⌒⊝—⊝⌒

A misprint in the church bulletin read: Our minister is leaving the church this Sunday. Will you please send in a small donation? The congregation wants to give him a little momentum.

⌒⊝—⊝⌒

Pastor: Yes, I know Mrs. Martin. She has been a corpse in our church for over thirty years.

CHURCH ATTENDERS

Dictionary of Church Attenders:
Pillars—worship regularly, giving time and money.
Leaners—use the church for funerals, baptisms, and marriages.
Specials—help and give occasionally for something that appeals to them.
Annuals—dress up for Easter and come for Christmas programs.
Sponges—take all blessings and benefits, even the sacraments, but never give out anything themselves.
Scrappers—take offense and criticize.

∾⊸—⊶∾

Some church members who say "Our Father" on Sunday go around the rest of the week acting like orphans.

CHURCH BULLETIN BOARDS

Come in and have your faith lifted.

∾⊸—⊶∾

Come in and let us prepare you for your finals.

∾⊸—⊶∾

A miser is a rich pauper.

∾⊸—⊶∾

Ask about our pray-as-you-go plan.

∾⊸—⊶∾

We hold sit-in demonstrations every Sunday.

Churchgoer

Q: What do you call a non-churchgoer?
A: A Seventh-Day Absentist.

Civil Servant

Q: What is the difference between a chess player and a civil servant?
A: A chess player moves every now and then.

Closing

Did you hear about the undertaker who closes all his letters with: "Eventually yours"?

Cold

"I have a cold or something in my head."
"I bet it's a cold."

Cold Cash

A woman's husband asked her what she wanted for her birthday the next week. She thought for a moment, then said, "This year I want cold, hard cash for a change."

The following day her husband filled her request. He put twenty dollars in nickels, dimes, and quarters into a quart jar, then filled it with water. On her birthday he handed his wife a solidly frozen bottle of change from the freezer.

Cold Cuts

"You're only as old as you think."
"In that case you must be about three months old."

Travel broadens a person. You look like you've been all over the world.

❀❀❀

I didn't say he was dumb—I said he was sixteen years old before he could wave good-bye.

❀❀❀

"Do you think I'm a fool?"
"No, but what's my opinion against thousands of others?"

❀❀❀

"Excuse me—I was lost in thought."
"Yes, it's always easy to get lost where one is a stranger."

❀❀❀

"Do you believe it is possible to communicate with the dead?"
"Yes, I can hear you distinctly."

❀❀❀

"I live by my wits."
"Now I know why you look so hungry."

❀❀❀

You have a striking personality. How long has it been on strike?

❀❀❀

You're not really such a bad person—until people get to know you.

❀❀❀

Of course I'm listening to you; don't you see me yawning?

❀❀❀

I've enjoyed talking to you; my mind needed the rest.

❧——☙

Is that your head, or did somebody find a way to grow hair on a meatball?

❧——☙

Ordinarily he was insane, but he had lucid moments when he was merely stupid.

❧——☙

I'd like to give you something you need, but I don't know how to wrap up a bathtub.

❧——☙

You talk so much I get hoarse just listening to you.

❧——☙

While he was not dumber than an ox, he was not any smarter either.

❧——☙

You really have a head on your shoulders. Too bad it's on backward.

❧——☙

You're such a bore, even my leg falls asleep when you talk.

❧——☙

Did I miss you when you were gone? I didn't know you were gone.

❧——☙

The only time you make sense is when you're not talking.

❧——❧

You may not be light on your feet, but you certainly are light in your head.

❧——❧

"What would the world be without its little joke?"
"You wouldn't be alive."

❧——❧

"They say two heads are better than one."
"In your case, none is better than one."

❧——❧

Things could be worse—you could be here in person.

❧——❧

You're a person of few words—a few million words.

❧——❧

There are two reasons why you don't mind your business: 1) no mind; and 2) no business.

❧——❧

Your face is familiar . . . I just can't recall which museum!

❧——❧

He should join the Ku Klux Klan—he'd look better with a hood over his face.

❧——❧

The only way she can get color in her face is to stick her tongue out.

⌒⊙⌒

He has a sympathetic face; it has everyone's sympathy.

⌒⊙⌒

She's not exactly bad looking. There's just a little blemish between her ears . . . her face.

⌒⊙⌒

Everyone says she's an angel fallen from the skies. Too bad she happened to land on her face.

⌒⊙⌒

Her face was so wrinkled she didn't dare wear long earrings—made her look like a Venetian blind.

⌒⊙⌒

Count to three; see if you can do it from memory.

⌒⊙⌒

She looks like she had her face lifted and the crane broke.

⌒⊙⌒

When I look at you, time stands still . . . what I really mean is that your face would stop a clock.

⌒⊙⌒

His trouble is too much bone in the head and not enough in the back.

⌒⊙⌒

He has a concrete mind . . . permanently set and all mixed up.

❦

He's a gross ignoramus . . . 144 times worse than an ordinary ignoramus.

❦

He's a man of rare intelligence . . . it's rare when he shows any.

❦

It's a mystery how his head grew without any nourishment.

❦

In your case, brain surgery would be a minor operation.

❦

What he lacks in intelligence he makes up for in stupidity.

❦

You could make a fortune renting your head out as a balloon.

❦

I wouldn't fret so much if I were you . . . after all, we can't all be mentally sound.

❦

Look, I'm not going to engage in a battle of wits with you . . . I never attack anyone who's unarmed.

❦

The only reason he manages to keep his head above water is that wood floats.

❦

He's an M.D . . . . Mentally Deficient.

◦⊖—⊖◦

Why don't you sue your brains for nonsupport?

◦⊖—⊖◦

She was hurt while taking a milk bath. The cow slipped and fell on her head.

◦⊖—⊖◦

I won't say she's narrow minded . . . but if it gets any worse she'll only have to use one earring.

◦⊖—⊖◦

He has a lot of backbone. The trouble is, the bone is all on the top.

◦⊖—⊖◦

You have a ready wit. Let me know when it's ready.

◦⊖—⊖◦

He's going to the hospital for a minor operation . . . they're putting a brain in.

◦⊖—⊖◦

My wife wants a vacuum for Christmas. Is your head available?

◦⊖—⊖◦

He's just as smart as he can be . . . unfortunately.

◦⊖—⊖◦

You'll make money someday. Your ignorance is comical.

◦⊖—⊖◦

He won't have to wait till he dies to be at his wit's end.

∽⊖—⊖∽

What's on your mind? . . . if you'll please excuse the exaggeration.

∽⊖—⊖∽

He should study to be a bone specialist. He has the head for it.

∽⊖—⊖∽

You know, there's a reason he's always got that stupid grin on his face: he's *stupid!*

∽⊖—⊖∽

He has an I.Q. just below plant life!

∽⊖—⊖∽

Generally speaking, she's generally speaking.

∽⊖—⊖∽

He has the awful flower disease . . . he's a blooming idiot!

∽⊖—⊖∽

Your mind will stay young . . . you use it so little!

∽⊖—⊖∽

He has a soft heart and a head to match!

∽⊖—⊖∽

I'm paid to make an idiot out of myself. Why do you do it for free?

∽⊖—⊖∽

He's not just an ordinary moron . . . he's a moron's moron.

⌁

Her vocabulary is small, but the turnover is terrific.

⌁

First thing in the morning, she brushes her teeth and sharpens her tongue.

⌁

She belongs to the meddle class.

⌁

She has a keen sense of rumor.

⌁

Listening to him makes you think of a river . . . small at the head and big at the mouth.

⌁

He must have goat glands . . . he's always butting in.

⌁

How can you talk all night without stopping to think?

⌁

If exercise eliminates fat, how in the world did you get that double chin?

⌁

You really have an open mind . . . and a mouth to match.

❧ — ☙

He carries pictures of the children and a soundtrack of his wife.

❧ — ☙

You could make a fortune if you could buy him for what you think of him and sell him for what he thinks of himself.

❧ — ☙

Their marriage is a partnership . . . he's the silent partner.

❧ — ☙

He's a second-story man; no one ever believes his first story.

❧ — ☙

He has such a big mouth he can eat a banana sideways, or sing duets by himself.

❧ — ☙

He sure has got a wide mouth for such a narrow mind.

❧ — ☙

Arguing with her is like trying to read a newspaper in a high wind.

❧ — ☙

Can she talk! She was in Miami and when she got home her tongue was sunburned.

❧ — ☙

When he meets another egotist, it's an I for an I.

⌒◦—◦⌒

He's always down on everything he's not up on.

⌒◦—◦⌒

He's an I-sore.

⌒◦—◦⌒

English is the mother tongue . . . because father seldom has a chance to use it.

⌒◦—◦⌒

She has a good memory—and a tongue hung in the middle of it.

⌒◦—◦⌒

Her tongue is so long she can seal an envelope after she puts it in the mailbox.

⌒◦—◦⌒

They call her "AT&T." . . . Always Talking and Talking.

⌒◦—◦⌒

She's so tired at the end of the day she can hardly keep her mouth open.

⌒◦—◦⌒

On his last birthday he sent his parents a telegram of congratulations.

⌒◦—◦⌒

He's suffering from I-dolatry.

⌒◦—◦⌒

If he had his life to live over again, he would still fall in love with himself.

⚬⊷—⊶⚬

He doesn't want anyone to make a fuss over him . . . just to treat him as they would any other great man.

⚬⊷—⊶⚬

She has such a sour look that when she puts on face cream it curdles.

⚬⊷—⊶⚬

She only has to go to the dentist twice a year . . . once for each tooth.

⚬⊷—⊶⚬

Be careful when you're speaking about him . . . you're speaking of the man he loves.

COLD GROUND

Was the ground cold when you crawled out this morning?

COLLECTION PLATE

One reason we have so many pennies in the church collection plate is because we have no smaller coin.

⚬⊷—⊶⚬

The minister arose to address his congregation. "There is a certain man among us today who is flirting with another man's wife. Unless he puts five dollars in the collection box, his name will be read from the pulpit."

When the collection plate came in, there were nineteen five-dollar bills, and a two-dollar bill with this note attached: "Other three on payday."

◦§——◦

A pastor wired all his pews with electricity. One Sunday from his pulpit he said, "All who will give one hundred dollars toward the new building, stand up." He touched a button, and twenty people sprang up.

"Fine, fine," the preacher beamed. "Now all who will give five hundred dollars, stand up." He touched another button and twenty more jumped to their feet.

"Excellent," he shouted. "Now all who will give one thousand dollars, stand up." He threw the master switch and electrocuted fifteen deacons.

◦§——◦

A church secretary answered the phone and heard the caller say, "I want to talk to the chief hog of the trough."

"Sir," she replied, "that is no way to talk about the Reverend. He is the pastor of this church."

"Sorry, lady," he said, "I just wanted to donate $100,000 to the church."

Quickly she said, "Just a minute. Here comes the big fat pig now."

◦§——◦

One beautiful Sunday morning, a minister announced to his congregation: "My good people, I have here in my hands three sermons—a one-hundred-dollar sermon that lasts five minutes, a fifty-dollar sermon that lasts fifteen minutes and a ten-dollar sermon that lasts a full hour. Now, we'll take the collection and see which one I'll deliver."

COLLEGE

Father: My son just received his B.A.
Neighbor: I suppose now he'll be looking for a Ph.D.
Father: No, now he's looking for a J.O.B.

◦§——◦

Letter from son at school:

Dear Dad,
Gue$$ what I need mo$t. That'$ right. $end it $oon.
Be$t Wi$he$
Jay

Reply:

Dear Jay,
NOthing ever happens here. We kNOw you like school. Write aNOther letter soon. Mom was asking about you at NOon.
NOw I have to say good-bye.
Dad

∽⊖—⊖∽

Professor to students: If you get this information in your brain, you will have it in a nutshell.

∽⊖—⊖∽

Professor: Give me three collective nouns.
Student: Flypaper, wastebasket, and vacuum cleaner.

∽⊖—⊖∽

A letter from a college student, "Please send food packages! All they serve here is breakfast, lunch, and dinner."

∽⊖—⊖∽

Neighbor: What is your son taking up at college?
Father: Space!

∽⊖—⊖∽

Professor: If there are any dumbbells in the room, please stand up.
(There was a long pause, then a lone freshman stood up in the rear.)
What? Do you consider yourself a dumbbell?
Freshman: Well, not exactly, but I hate to see you standing all alone.

∽⊖—⊖∽

President of the college: Are you a student here?
Student: No, I just go to college here.

❦

Student: Professor, my opinion of you is most contemptible.
Professor: Sir, I never knew an opinion of yours that was not contemptible.

❦

Student: I hear that fish is brain food.
Roommate: Yeah, I eat it all the time.
Student: Well, there goes another theory.

❦

Tony: My college has turned out some great men.
Daisy: I didn't know you were a college graduate.
Tony: I'm the one they turned out!

❦

First father: What's your boy going to be when he finishes college?
Second father: An octogenarian.

❦

The greatest aid to adult education is children.

❦

College student with coin in his hand: "If it's heads, I go to bed. If it's tails, I stay up. If it stands on edge, I study."

COLLEGE CHEER

Money from home.

❦

Two editors of local newspapers did not get along and used their newspapers to do battle.

"The big editor of the *Daily Express* is mean enough to steal the swill from a blind hog," wrote the editor of the *Daily Post*.

The next day the following appeared in the *Daily Express*:

"The editor of the *Daily Post* knows that we never stole his swill."

COMEDIAN

A person who has a good memory for old jokes.

COMPUTERS

If computers get too powerful, we can organize them into committees. That'll do them in.

~⌇—⌇~

"I've invented a computer that's almost human."

"You mean, it can think?"

"No. But when it makes a mistake it can put the blame on another computer."

CONCENTRATE

Member: Pastor, how did you get that cut on your face?

Pastor: I was thinking about my sermon this morning and wasn't concentrating on what I was doing, and I cut myself while shaving.

Member: That's too bad! Next time you had better concentrate on your shaving and cut your sermon!

CONSCIENCE

Mark Twain used to tell the story of how he once stole a watermelon from a cart when the owner was not looking. He carried the melon to a secret spot, sat down, and was just about to bite into the melon when he realized that he should not do that. It just wasn't right.

So, he got up, took the watermelon back, replaced it on the cart, and took a ripe one.

Cooking

Bride: The two best things I cook are meatloaf and apple dumplings.
Groom: Well, which is this?

◦◦—◦◦

"Some people can cook but don't."
"My wife can't cook but does."

◦◦—◦◦

A sorely pressed newlywed sought valiantly to console his little bride, who sprawled, dissolved in tears, on the chaise lounge. "Darling," he implored, "believe me. I never said you were a terrible cook. I merely pointed out that our garbage disposal has developed an ulcer."

◦◦—◦◦

New bride: I fixed your favorite dessert for you tonight—coconut pudding. Wait until you see it.
New groom: Wow! That's great! But what's that big lump in the middle?
New bride: That's the coconut.

◦◦—◦◦

First husband: When I'm near death, I'll ask my wife to cook my last meal.
Second husband: Why?
First husband: I'll feel more like dying.

Countdown

Overheard at the rocket launchpad control room: "He's a fine fellow practically all of the time, but he is inclined to blow-up without any countdown."

Court

Judge: Have you a lawyer?
Prisoner: No, but I have some good friends on the jury.

❦

"Will you tell the court how far you were taken from the spot where the shooting occurred?" asked the defense counsel.

"I was exactly fourteen feet, three-and-one-half inches," replied the witness.

"How can you be sure of the exact distance?" asked the lawyer.

"I measured it because I was sure sooner or later some fool would ask that question."

❦

The judge was cross-examining a colonel. Unable to shake his testimony he tried sarcasm. "They call you colonel. In what regiment are you a colonel?" "Well," drawled the colonel, "It's like this. The 'Colonel' in front of my name is like the 'Honorable' in front of yours. It doesn't mean a thing."

❦

The district attorney was cross-examining the murderess.

"And after you had poisoned the coffee and your husband sat at the breakfast table partaking of the fatal dosage, didn't you feel any qualms? Didn't you feel the slightest pity for him, knowing he was about to die and was wholly unaware of it?"

"Yes, there was a moment when I sort of felt sorry for him."

"When was that?"

"When he asked for the second cup."

Cow

A man's car stalled on a country road. When he got out to fix it, a cow came along and stopped beside him. "Your trouble is probably in the carburetor," said the cow.

Startled, the man jumped back and ran down the road until he met the farmer. He told the farmer his story.

"Was it a large red cow with a brown spot over the right eye?" asked the farmer.

"Yes, yes," the man replied.

"Oh! I wouldn't listen to Bessie," said the farmer. "She doesn't know anything about cars."

CRAZY

Patient: Doctor, people are always calling me crazy. It makes me very angry.

Psychiatrist: Perhaps you ought to start at the beginning. . . .

Patient: Okay. In the beginning, I created the heavens and the earth. And the earth was without form and void. . . .

∽⊙—⊙∾

A man pleaded with the psychiatrist, "You've got to help me. It's my son."

"What's the matter?"

"He's always eating mud pies. I get up in the morning and there he is in the backyard eating mud pies. I come home at lunch and he is eating mud pies. I come home at dinner and there he is in the backyard eating mud pies."

The psychiatrist reassured him, "Give the kid a chance. It's all part of growing up. It'll pass."

"Well, I don't like it, and neither does his wife."

∽⊙—⊙∾

One out of four Americans is mentally ill. Next time you're in a group of four people, take a good look at the other three. If they look all right, you're it!

∽⊙—⊙∾

The only reason we invited him here tonight is to remind you that every sixty seconds mental illness strikes!

∾⊖—⊖∾

Husband: My wife talks to herself—she must be insane.

Psychiatrist: Ridiculous. You wouldn't be insane just because you talked to yourself.

Husband: No?

Psychiatrist: Of course not. I talk to myself. Do you think I'm insane?

Husband: I wouldn't say you're insane if you talked to yourself. But you would be if you listened.

∾⊖—⊖∾

A psychiatrist was trying to comfort a new patient who was terribly upset. "You see, Doc," the patient explained, "my problem is that I like shoes much better than I like boots."

"Why, that's no problem," answered the doctor. "Most people like shoes better than boots."

The patient was elated. "That's neat, Doc. How do you like them, fried or scrambled?"

∾⊖—⊖∾

An important official who was visiting an insane asylum made a telephone call but had difficulty getting his number. Finally, in exasperation, he shouted to the operator, "Look here, girl, do you know who I am?"

"No," she replied calmly, "but I know where you are."

∾⊖—⊖∾

A motorist had a flat tire in front of the insane asylum. He took the wheel off, and the bolts that held the wheel on rolled down into the sewer.

An inmate, looking through the fence, suggested that the man take one bolt from each of the remaining three wheels to hold the fourth wheel in place until he could get to a service station.

The motorist thanked him profusely and said, "I don't know why you are in that place."

The inmate said, "I'm here for being crazy, not for being stupid."

CRAZY, MAN, CRAZY

Today more and more hippies are looking to religion for the answer to their problems. Last Sunday, a hippie went to church and was so overwhelmed by the sermon he grabbed the preacher's hand when he left the church and said, "Dad, I read you: that sermon was the most; it was gone; you were right on." The preacher said, "I'm afraid I don't understand." The hippie said, "Yes, you do, dad. In fact I liked it so gone, I put twenty samolas in the collection plate." The preacher said, "Oh, crazy, man, crazy."

CRIME

We don't seem to be able to check crime, so why not legalize it and then tax it out of business?
—*Will Rogers*

❧——❧

There's so much crime in my neighborhood the intersection lights say, "Shoot," and, "Don't shoot."

CRITICIZE

When the family returned from Sunday morning service, father criticized the sermon, daughter thought the choir's singing was off-key, and mother found fault with the organist's playing. The subject had to be dropped when the small boy of the family said, "But it was a good show for a nickel, don't you think, Dad?"

CROSSWORD PUZZLE

Did you hear about the crossword puzzle addict who died and was buried six feet down and three feet across?

CURIOSITY

A sharp nose indicates curiosity. A flattened nose indicates too much curiosity.

CUTIE PIE

One afternoon the boss's wife met him at the office. As they were going down the elevator, it stopped, and a luscious blonde secretary got on, poked the boss in the ribs, and said, "Hello, cutie pie."

The wife, without blinking, leaned over and said, "I'm Mrs. Pie."

⊰ D ⊱

Daffy Definitions

ADMIRATION: Our polite recognition of another person's resemblance to ourselves.

❧ ——— ☙

ADOLESCENCE: The period in which the young suddenly feel a great responsibility about answering the telephone.

❧ ——— ☙

ADOLESCENCE: The period when children are certain they will never be as dumb as their parents.

❧ ——— ☙

ADOLESCENT: A teenager who acts like a baby when you don't treat him like an adult.

❧ ——— ☙

AMERICANS: People with more timesaving devices and less time than any other people in the world.

❧ ——— ☙

ANTIDOTE: The medicine that kills dotes.

❧ ——— ☙

BACHELOR: A rolling stone that gathers no boss.

❧ ——— ☙

BANKER: A fellow who lends you his umbrella when the sun is shining and wants it back the minute it begins to rain.

❦

BANKER: A pawnbroker with a manicure.

❦

BORE: Someone who, upon leaving a room, makes you feel that someone fascinating just walked in.

❦

BUDGET: A method of worrying before you spend as well as afterward.

❦

BUDGET: A schedule for going into debt systematically.

❦

BUDGET: An attempt to live below your yearnings.

❦

BUS FARE: Jack-in-the-box.

❦

CLARITY: The ability to give directions without taking your hands out of your pockets.

❦

COACH: A fellow who is always willing to lay down your life for his job.

❦

CRITIC: A legless man who teaches running.

❦

DENTIST: A magician who puts metal into your mouth, and pulls coins out of your pocket.

❦

DERMATOLOGIST: A person who makes rash judgments.

❦

DIPLOMACY: The art of saying "nice doggie" until you have time to pick up a rock.

❦

DISARMAMENT: An agreement between nations to scuttle all weapons that are obsolete.

❦

ECONOMIST: A man who knows more about money than people who have it.

❦

EFFICIENCY EXPERT: The person who is smart enough to tell you how to run your business and too smart to start one of his own.

❦

ELOCUTION: A form of punishment whereby many people are put to death.

❦

ETERNAL TRIANGLES: Diapers.

❦

EXPERIENCE: The name we give our mistakes.

∽⊖—⊖∾

FLATTERY: A collection of flats.

∽⊖—⊖∾

FRIENDSHIP: An emotion so sweet, steady, loyal, and enduring that it lasts an entire lifetime—unless asked to lend money.

∽⊖—⊖∾

FURTHERMORE: It is much farther than "further."

∽⊖—⊖∾

HONEYMOON: The vacation a man takes before beginning work under a new boss.

∽⊖—⊖∾

HOSPITAL BED: A parked taxi with the meter running.

∽⊖—⊖∾

HUNCH: What you call an idea that you're afraid is wrong.

∽⊖—⊖∾

IGNORAMUS: Someone who doesn't know something that you learned yesterday.

∽⊖—⊖∾

INCENTIVE: The possibility of getting more money than you earn.

∽⊖—⊖∾

INSOMNIA: What a person has when he lies awake all night for an hour.

$\sim\!\!\circ\!\!-\!\!\circ\!\!\sim$

INSURANCE: Paying for catastrophes on the installment plan.

$\sim\!\!\circ\!\!-\!\!\circ\!\!\sim$

ITALICS: The language spoken by ancient Italians.

$\sim\!\!\circ\!\!-\!\!\circ\!\!\sim$

LAME DUCK: A politician whose goose has been cooked.

$\sim\!\!\circ\!\!-\!\!\circ\!\!\sim$

LIFE INSURANCE: A contract that keeps you poor so you can die rich.

$\sim\!\!\circ\!\!-\!\!\circ\!\!\sim$

MARKET ANALYST: A person who tells you what is going to happen within six months and then after that tells you why it didn't.

$\sim\!\!\circ\!\!-\!\!\circ\!\!\sim$

METALLURGIST: Someone who is allergic to iron.

$\sim\!\!\circ\!\!-\!\!\circ\!\!\sim$

NURSERY: A school for nurses.

$\sim\!\!\circ\!\!-\!\!\circ\!\!\sim$

ORATORY: The art of making deep noises from the chest sound like important messages from the brain.

$\sim\!\!\circ\!\!-\!\!\circ\!\!\sim$

PACIFIST: A guy who fights with everybody but the enemy.

◈

PANTRY: A collection of pants.

◈

PAST TENSE: When you used to be nervous.

◈

PAWNBROKER: One who lives off the flat of the land.

◈

PEDIATRICIANS: Men of little patients.

◈

PLANNING: The art of putting off until tomorrow what you have no intention of doing today.

◈

PROFESSOR: One who talks in someone else's sleep.

◈

QUININE: A valuable medicine that comes from barking trees.

◈

RELATIVITY: When you are with a pretty girl for three hours, and it seems like only three minutes, and then you sit on a hot stove for a minute and think it's an hour.

◈

RICH MAN: One who isn't afraid to ask the clerk to show him something cheaper.

SARCASM: Barbed ire.

SINKING FUND: A place where they hide the profits from the stockholders.

SPECIALIST: A doctor whose patients are expected to confine their ailments to his office hours.

STATISTICIAN: A liar who can figure.

STOCKBROKER: A man who can take a bankroll and run it into a shoestring.

TACT: Thinking all you say without saying all you think.

TACT: The art of saying nothing when there is nothing to say.

TAXPAYER: One who doesn't have to pass a civil service exam to work for the government.

UPPER CRUST: A lot of crumbs held together by dough.

∾⊙—⊙∾

UNIVERSITY: An institution for the postponement of experience.

∾⊙—⊙∾

WAITER: A man who thinks money grows on trays.

∾⊙—⊙∾

YAWN: A silent shout.

∾⊙—⊙∾

ZOO: A place devised for animals to study the habits of human beings.

Debt

A man who was late in paying his bills received the following note: "Your account has been on our books for over a year. Just want to remind you we have now carried you longer than your mother did."

∾⊙—⊙∾

"Would you be happy if you had all the money you wanted?"
"I'd be happy if I had all the money my creditors wanted."

∾⊙—⊙∾

Glen: Are you still living within your income?
Rich: No. It's all I can do to live within my credit.

∾⊙—⊙∾

Here it is in the middle of January and we're still cleaning up from Christmas. Last week we cleaned out our checking account; this week we cleaned out our savings account.

Deep Water

When you are in deep water, it's a good idea to keep your mouth shut.

Degrees

A girl at Bennington named Louise
Weighed down with Ph.D.'s and D.D.'s
Collapsed from the strain
Said her doctor, "It's plain
You are killing yourself—by degrees."

Dentist

Dentist: Good grief! You've got the biggest cavity I've ever seen—the biggest cavity I've ever seen.
Patient: You don't have to repeat it, doc!
Dentist: I didn't—that was the echo.

∽๏—๏∾

Dentist: Do you want the good news or the bad news?
Patient: Give me the good news.
Dentist: Your teeth are perfect.
Patient: What's the bad news?
Dentist: Your gums are so bad that I'll have to take all your teeth out.

∽๏—๏∾

George was having trouble with a toothache, so he decided to visit the dentist.
"What do you charge for extracting a tooth?" George asked.
"Five dollars," replied the dentist.
"Five dollars for only two minutes' work?" exclaimed George.
"Well," replied the dentist, "if you wish, I can extract it very slowly."

Deviled Ham

Q: Where was deviled ham mentioned in the Bible?
A: When the evil spirits entered the swine.

Diet

You know it is time for a diet when:
You dive into a swimming pool so her friends can go surfing.
You have to apply your makeup with a paint roller.
Weight Watchers demands your resignation.
You step on a pennyweight scale that gives you your fortune and it says, "One at a time, please!"
Your face is so full that you look like you're wearing horn-rimmed contact lenses.
The bus driver asks you to sit on the other side because he wants to make a turn without flipping over.
You're at school in the classroom and turn around and erase the entire blackboard.
They throw puffed rice at your wedding.
You get a hiccup while in your bathing suit . . . and it looks like someone adjusting a Venetian blind.
You fall down and try to get up, rocking yourself to sleep in the process.
A shipbuilder wants to use you as a model.

❧——❧

A diet is a short period of starvation preceding a gain of five pounds.

❧——❧

A diet is what helps a person gain weight more slowly.

❧——❧

She: I've got a new diet that is guaranteed to make you lose weight . . . and you can eat anything you want.

He: You mean eat anything I want?
She: Yes, but don't swallow.

DIFFERENCE

Teacher: What's the difference between a porpoise and a dolphin?
Student: That's what I say. What's the difference?

DINNER JACKET

Did you read where Liberace had a sequined dinner jacket made up that cost him $3,000? Isn't that ridiculous? Anyone who pays more than $2,000 for a dinner jacket is plain crazy!

DIRECTIONS

If at first you don't succeed, try looking in the wastebasket for the directions.

DISCUSSION

Angry wife to husband: No! Every time we discuss something sensibly, I lose!

DIVORCE

"Have you ever thought about divorcing your wife?"
"Divorce? . . . No. Murder? . . . Yes!"

DOCTOR

Dr. Hanson: So the operation on the man was just in the nick of time?
Dr. Poure: Yes, in another twenty-four hours he would have recovered.

A lady with a pain in her side went to see a doctor. He told her she had appendicitis and must have an operation. She decided to get another doctor's opinion. The second doctor told her she had heart trouble. "I'm going back to the first doctor," she replied. "I'd rather have appendicitis."

❦

A doctor was called in to see a very busy patient. "Well, sir, what's the matter?" he asked cheerfully.

"That's for you to find out," the patient snapped.

"I see," said the doctor. "Well, if you'll excuse me a minute, I'll phone a friend of mine—a veterinarian. He's the only man I know who can make a diagnosis without asking questions."

❦

Nurse: Doctor, there's a man in the waiting room who claims he's invisible.

Doctor: Tell him I can't see him.

❦

My doctor is an eye, ear, nose, throat, and wallet specialist.

❦

My husband, a marriage counselor, often refuses to accompany me to parties and get-togethers. He says that so many people spoil his evening by asking him for advice. One day I saw my doctor and I asked him if this happened to him also. He told me that it happened to him all the time. I then asked him how he got rid of those people.

"I have a wonderful remedy," the doctor grinned. "When someone begins to tell me his ailments, I stop him with one word: 'Undress.'"

❦

My wife was very sick so we called Dr. Griffin. He gave her some medicine and she got worse. I then called Dr. Kurth and he gave her some more medicine and she still got worse. I thought she was going to die, so I called Dr. Cross and he was too busy, and finally my wife got well.

∽—∾

My doctor is a very generous man. He gave me four months to live. When I told him that I didn't think I would be able to pay his bill before I died, he gave me another six months.

∽—∾

Patient: Doctor, I've got trouble with my throat.
Doctor: Go in the other room and disrobe. I'll be there in a minute.
Patient: But, doctor, it's just my throat!
Doctor: Get in the other room and disrobe and I'll examine you.
So the man went in and disrobed. As he was sitting there in his shorts, he looked around. Next to him was another guy sitting there in his shorts also, with a big package in his hands.
Patient: Can you imagine that doctor! I've got trouble with my throat and he tells me to disrobe!
Other man: What are you complaining about? I only came in here to deliver a package.

∽—∾

Mr. Jones phoned the doctor for an appointment. The nurse said she could give him an appointment in two weeks.
"In two weeks I could be dead!" wailed Jones.
"Well, in that case," answered the nurse, "you can always cancel the appointment!"

∽—∾

Sam: Why do doctors and nurses wear masks?
Pete: So that if someone makes a mistake no one will know who did it.

∽—∾

Did you hear about the man who swallowed his glass eye and rushed to a stomach specialist? The specialist peered down the unfortunate fellow's throat and exclaimed, "I've looked into a lot of stomachs in my day, but I must say, this is the first one that ever looked back at me."

∽⟶⟶⟵

Doctors keep telling us to get lots of fresh air, but they never tell us where to find it.

DOCTORS' BILLS

On his sixth call following a dangerous operation, the doctor was surprised to hear the patient say: "Doctor, I am feeling so much better. I want you to let me have your bill."

"Nonsense, my good man," replied the physician. "You are far from strong enough for that."

∽⟶⟶⟵

Doctor: I can do nothing for your sickness. It is hereditary.
Patient: Then send the bill to my father.

∽⟶⟶⟵

Doctor: Just do as I say, and you'll be another man.
Patient: Okay, and Doctor, don't forget to send your bill to the other man.

∽⟶⟶⟵

Gary: Only last week they took my poor brother off to the hospital.
Larry: What are they going to do for him?
Gary: They're going to operate.
Larry: What for?
Gary: Twelve hundred dollars.
Larry: What did he have?
Gary: Twelve hundred dollars.

Larry: What was the complaint?
Gary: No complaint. Everybody was satisfied.

❧——☙

Patient: Doc, what's the difference between an itch and an allergy?
Doctor: About thirty-five dollars.

Dog

Outside a house in Sussex, England: Beware of owner. Never mind the dog.

❧——☙

A man tried to sell his neighbor a new dog.

"This is a talking dog," he said. "And you can have him for five dollars."

The neighbor said, "Who do you think you're kidding with this talking dog stuff? There ain't no such animal."

Suddenly the dog looked up with tears in his eyes. "Please buy me, sir," he pleaded. "This man is cruel. He never buys me a meal, never bathes me, never takes me for a walk. And I used to be the richest trick dog in America. I performed before kings. I was in the Army and was decorated ten times."

"Hey!" said the neighbor. "He can talk. Why do you want to sell him for just five dollars?"

"Because," said the seller, "I'm getting tired of all his lies."

❧——☙

Did you hear about the dog who played Bach? He was about to be auditioned by a TV producer. The dog's agent warned the producer that this was a very sensitive dog, and that "you had better listen to him play because, if you don't, he loses his temper and leaps at you."

The dog started to play. He was awful. The TV producer patiently waited out the performance. When it was over, he declared angrily, "I should have let him attack. I'm sure his Bach is worse than his bite."

❧——☙

A man answered his doorbell and a friend walked in, followed by a very large dog. As they began talking, the dog knocked over a lamp and jumped up on the sofa with his muddy feet and began chewing on one of the pillows.

The outraged householder, unable to contain himself any longer, burst out, "Don't you think you should train your dog better?"

"*My* dog!" exclaimed the friend, surprised. "I thought it was *your* dog."

Donkey

One day some soldiers from a nearby Army camp saw a boy leading a donkey. They thought they would have some fun with him.

"Say, boy," called out one of the soldiers. "You sure are keeping a tight rein on your brother, aren't you?"

"I sure am," said the boy. "If I didn't he would probably join the Army."

Double Take

Life's briefest moment is the time between reading the sign on the freeway and realizing you just missed your exit.

Driving

A man who was driving an auto with his wife in the back seat stalled his car on a railroad track. A train was coming down the track. His wife screamed, "Go on! Go on!"

The husband responded, "You've been driving all day from the back seat. I've got my end across the track. See what you can do with your end."

∽⚬–⚬∾

To be honest, there are number of red lights that I have driven through. But on the other hand, I've stopped at a lot of green lights that I've never gotten credit for.

DULL

It is always dullest just before the yawn.

∽⊖─⊖∼

The trouble with telling a good story is that it reminds the other fellow of a dull one.

∽⊖─⊖∼

The dull thing about taking the straight and narrow path is that you so seldom meet anybody you know.

∽⊖─⊖∼

DUMB

I didn't say he was dumb . . . I said he was twenty years old before he could wave good-bye.

DUST

On the way home from church a little boy asked his mother, "Is it true, Mommy, that we are made of dust?"

"Yes, darling."

"And do we go back to dust again when we die?"

"Yes, dear."

"Well, Mommy, when I said my prayers last night and looked under the bed, I found someone who is either coming or going."

⊰ E ⊱

Easel

An artist decided to buy a new easel. He wasn't too sure what type to get. At the art shop they offered him two, a big one and a small one. He pondered for a while and finally decided on the lesser of two easels.

Editor

A person employed on a newspaper, whose business is to separate the wheat from the chaff—and see that the chaff is printed.

Egypt

Gary: A man just sold me the Nile River.
Larry: Egypt you.

Elephant

Christy: What's the difference between an elephant and a matterbaby?
Mark: What's a matterbaby?
Christy: Nothing. I didn't know you cared.

❦

Harry: Why did the elephant paint his toenails different colors?
Cary: I don't know.
Harry: So he could hide in the M&M's.

❦

One day a large elephant saw a turtle near a pond. The elephant lumbered over and squashed the turtle under its large foot.

A jackal who saw the murder ran over to the elephant and said, "Why did you do that?"

The elephant replied, "this is the same turtle that bit the tip of my trunk seventeen years ago, when I went to get a drink out of the river."

The jackal's eyes widened. "The same one? You must have an incredible memory!"

Raising its head proudly, the elephant said, "Turtle recall."

✎—✑

A man was waiting at an intersection for a circus to pass by. He saw a sign on one of the wagons that read: "Barney's Circus with Fifty Elephants." He counted the elephants as they crossed the intersection. When he got to fifty, he put his car in gear and started to cross the intersection because he was late for an appointment. Unfortunately, he had miscounted and his car hit and killed the last elephant.

A week later he got a notice from the circus that he'd have to pay $200,000. He called the circus manager and inquired, "What's the deal? I only hit one lousy elephant! Why do you want $200,000?"

The manager responded, "It's true, you only hit one elephant, but you pulled the tails out of forty-nine others!"

EMBARRASS

Two girls boarded a crowded bus and one of them whispered to the other, "Watch me embarrass a man into giving me his seat."

Pushing her way through the crowd, she turned all her charms upon a gentleman who looked like he might embarrass easily. "My dear Mr. Wilson," she gushed, "fancy meeting on the bus. Am I glad to see you. Why, you're almost a stranger. My, but I'm tired."

The sedate gentleman looked up at the girl. He had never seen her before but he rose and said pleasantly, "Sit down, Mary, my girl. It isn't often I see you on washday. No wonder you're tired. Being pregnant isn't easy. By the way, don't deliver the wash until Thursday. My wife is going to the District Attorney's office to see whether she can get your husband out of jail."

ENJOYABLE

For a minute I didn't recognize you. It was my most enjoyable minute today.

ETHICS

Son: Dad, what is ethics?

Dad: Well, son, you know that your uncle and I are in business together. Suppose a customer comes in and buys something worth ten dollars but by mistake gives me a twenty dollar bill and leaves without waiting for his change. If I split the extra ten dollars with your uncle, that's ethics.

EVOLUTION

I haven't much doubt that man sprang from the monkey, but where did the monkey spring from?

∾⊙—☾∾

Q: How many evolutionists does it take to screw in a light bulb?

A: Just one, but it takes him 200,000 years.

EXCUSES

Jones came into the office an hour late for the third time in one week and found the boss waiting for him. "What's the story this time, Jones?" he asked sarcastically. "Let's hear a good excuse for a change."

Jones sighed, "Everything went wrong this morning, boss. The wife decided to drive me to the station. She got ready in ten minutes, but then the drawbridge got stuck. Rather than let you down, I swam across the river (look, my suit's still damp), ran out to the airport, got a ride on Mr. Thompson's helicopter, landed on top of Radio City Music Hall, and was carried here piggyback by one of the Rockettes."

"You'll have to do better than that, Jones," said the boss, obviously disappointed. "No woman can be ready in ten minutes."

∾⊙—☾∾

One day an employee arrived late with one eye closed, his left arm in a sling, and his clothes in tatters. "It's 9:30," pointed out the president, "and you were due at 8:30." The employee explained, "I fell out of a tenth-story window." The president snorted, "It took you a whole hour?"

EXPERIENCE

Experience is the thing you have left when everything else is gone.

EYE CHART

"Simply read the letters on that chart," ordered the draft board doctor.

"I don't see any chart," answered the draftee happily.

"You're absolutely right," snapped the doctor. "There isn't any chart. "You're 1–A."

❈ F ❈

FACE

Nit: Haven't I seen your face somewhere else?
Wit: I don't think so. It has always been between my ears.

FALLS

Pam: I fell off a sixty-foot ladder today.
Melba: It's a miracle you weren't killed.
Pam: Oh, I only fell off the first rung.

❧ ⸻ ❧

Rob: What is four yards long, has six legs, and would kill you if it fell out of a tree?
Ted: I don't know.
Rob: A billiard table.

FALSE TEETH

At a Sunday school picnic the minister, who was walking across a small footbridge, was seized with a fit of sneezing. His false teeth flew from his mouth and landed in the clear water in the middle of the stream. Much worried and embarrassed, the minister was preparing to remove his shoes and wade in after his dentures when a dear little gray-haired grandmother appeared on the scene, carrying a well-filled dinner basket. When she discovered the minister's plight, she reached in her basket, removed a crisp, brown chicken leg, tied a string to it and tossed it into the water near the dentures. Quickly the teeth clamped into the chicken leg and were hauled to safety.

FAMILY

The average American family consists of 4.1 persons. You have one guess as to who constitutes the .1 person.

❦

I have been told that insanity is hereditary. Parents get it from their children.

FAMOUS LAST WORDS

"You can make it easily—that train isn't coming fast."

❦

"Gimme a match. I think my gas tank is empty."

❦

"Wife, these biscuits are tough."

❦

"Let's see if it's loaded."

❦

"Step on her, boy, we're only going seventy-five."

FARMER

A man traveling through the country stopped at a small fruit stand and bought some apples. When he commented they were awfully small, the farmer replied, "Yup."

The man took a bite of one of the apples and exclaimed, "Not very flavorful, either."

"That's right," said the farmer. "Lucky they're small, ain't it?"

⚬—⚬

One Sunday as a farmer was getting in his hay crop, his minister stopped by. The pastor asked the farmer if he had been to church. "To tell the truth, I would rather sit on the hay load and think about the church than sit in the church and think about hay."

⚬—⚬

Ralph: Down on our farm, we had a hen lay an egg six inches long.
John: That's nothing. On our farm we can beat that.
Ralph: How?
John: With an egg beater.

⚬—⚬

Did you hear about the farmer who decided to buy a chain saw? A logging foreman sold him one that he guaranteed would cut down fifteen trees in a single day. A week later, a very unhappy farmer came back to report that the power saw must be faulty—it averaged only three trees a day. The foreman grabbed the saw, pulled the cord, and the saw promptly went, "Bzzzzzzzzzzz."
"Hey," demanded the startled farmer, "what's that noise?"

⚬—⚬

A motorist, after being bogged down in a muddy road, paid a passing farmer five dollars to pull him out with his tractor. After he was back on dry ground he said to the farmer, "At those prices, I should think you would be pulling people out of the mud night and day."
"Can't," replied the farmer. "At night I haul water for the hole."

FATHER'S DAY

First wife: How would you describe Father's Day?
Second wife: Just like Mother's Day . . . only you don't spend as much money.

FICTIONAL

Note from writer to editor: The characters in this novel are entirely fictional and have no resemblance to any person living or dead.

Note from editor to writer: That's what is wrong with them.

FIRST HUSBAND

The grief-stricken man threw himself across the grave and cried bitterly. "My life, how senseless it is! How worthless is everything about me because you are gone. If only you hadn't died, if only fate had not been so cruel as to take you from this world, how different everything would have been."

A clergyman happened by and to soothe the man he offered a prayer. Afterward he said, "I assume the person lying beneath this mound of earth was someone of importance to you."

"Importance? Indeed it was," moaned the man. "It's my wife's first husband!"

FISHING

Customer: Do you have any cockroaches?
Sporting goods store owner: Yes, we sell them to fishermen.
Customer: I would like 20,000 of them.
Sporting goods store owner: What do you want with 20,000 cockroaches?
Customer: I'm moving tomorrow and my lease says I must leave my apartment in the condition in which I found it.

❧ ❧

Stranger: Catch any fish?
Fisherman: Did I? I took thirty out of this stream this morning.
Stranger: Do you know who I am? I'm the game warden.
Fisherman: Do you know who I am? I'm the biggest liar in the country.

❧ ❧

A certain man had a great reputation for always catching his limit of fish. Everyone wanted to know his secret. One day the game warden asked to go along to see where he was fishing.

The man and the game warden got into a boat and rowed to the middle of a nearby lake. The fisherman threw over an anchor, and then reached into a paper sack. He pulled out a stick of dynamite, lit a match to the fuse, and tossed it onto the lake. There was a huge explosion and several fish floated to the surface.

The game warden was irate. He yelled, "You can't do that! It's against the law!"

The fisherman then reached into the sack and pulled out another stick of dynamite. He lit the fuse and then threw it into the lap of the game warden. As he did this he asked, "Are you going to talk or fish?"

⚬―⚬

Game Warden: Fishing?
Man without license: No, drowning worms.

FIT FOR A PIG

Customer: This food isn't fit for a pig!
Waiter: I'm sorry, sir. I'll bring you some that is.

FLIRTING

Peggy: I caught my boyfriend flirting.
Sharon: Yes, that's the way I caught mine, too.

FLYSWATTER

Little Billy was left to fix lunch. When his mother returned with a friend, she noticed that Billy had already strained the tea.

"Did you find the tea strainer?" his mother asked.

"No mother, I couldn't, so I used the flyswatter," replied Billy.

His mother nearly fainted, so Billy hastily added, "Don't get excited, Mother. I used an old one."

Food

Rich: What are you eating?
Dave: Calves' brains and oxtail soup.
Rich: That's one way of making ends meet.

❧——❧

I have finally found out why babies suck their thumbs. I tried some of the baby food.

Fool

Rev. Henry Ward Beecher received a letter with one word written on it. It said, "Fool." The next Sunday he read the letter from the pulpit and said, "I have received many letters from people who have forgotten to sign their names, but this is the first time I've received a letter from someone who signed his name but forgot to write the letter."

Football

First mother: What position does your son play on the football team?
Second mother: I'm not sure. I think he's one of the drawbacks.

❧——❧

"I was injured on the football team."
"How?"
"I fell off the bench."

❧——❧

During the review of the football plays before a big game, one of the star running backs spent most of the time reading a comic book. The coach noticed but didn't say anything about it.

It was a very exciting and important game, but the coach made the running back sit on the bench until the last quarter. When the last quarter started the coach said to the running back, "Warm up!"

After a series of warm-up moves, the running back said, "I'm ready, coach."

The coach reached into his coat pocket and pulled out a comic book. "Here," he said. "Sit over there at the end of the bench and read it."

FORK

If you drop a fork, it's a sign company is coming. If a fork is missing, it's a sign company is going.

⊰ G ⊱

GALAXIES

NASA reports that galaxies are speeding away from earth at 90,000 miles a second. What do you suppose they know that we don't?

GARAGE SALE

A garage sale is a technique for distributing all the junk in your garage among all the other garages in the neighborhood.

GARDENING

"What are you doing?"
"I'm watering my beans."
"But there is no water coming out of the can."
"Do you see any beans?"

◦◦—◦◦

When it comes to gardening, there's no better labor-saving device than a bad back.

GAS

"Hello! Is this the City Gas Works?"
"No, this is the Mayor's office."
"Well, I didn't miss it very far, did I?"

GAS SAVER

I have been having some trouble with the new car I bought. I added a carburetor that saved thirty percent on gas, a timer that saved fifty percent on gas, and spark plugs that saved thirty percent on gas. I drove ten miles and the gas tank overflowed.

GENERATION

Little girl: Mother, you know that vase you said had been handed down from generation to generation?
Mother: Yes.
Little girl: Well, this generation just dropped it.

GETTING MARRIED

Attorney: You knew he was a burglar when you married him?
Woman: Yes.
Attorney: May I ask how you came to marry such an individual?
Woman: You may. You see I was getting older and had to choose between marrying a burglar or a lawyer.

∽⊝—⊖∾

A couple in Hollywood got divorced, then got remarried. The divorce didn't work out.

∽⊝—⊖∾

Bride: I don't want to forget any insignificant details.
Mother: Don't worry! I'll be sure he's there!

∽⊝—⊖∾

A newly married couple was checking into a hotel-resort. They asked the clerk at the desk to keep their newlywed status a secret.

The next morning the newlyweds were aware of being stared at when they headed for the diner. The groom was very angry and sought out the man at the desk. He rebuked him for passing on the word that they had just been married.

"I never told them at all," said the clerk. "I just said that you two were good friends."

∽⊝—⊖∾

Two married girls were bothering a third girl who was still a spinster.

"Now, tell us truthfully," they badgered her, "have you ever really had a chance to marry?"

With a withering glance, she retorted, "Suppose you ask your husbands."

GHOST

A photographer went to a haunted castle determined to get a picture of a ghost which was said to appear only once in a hundred years. Not wanting to frighten off the spook, the photographer sat in the dark until midnight when the apparition became visible.

The ghost turned out to be friendly and consented to pose for a snapshot. The happy photographer popped a bulb into his camera and took the picture. Then he dashed to his studio, developed the negative . . . and groaned. It was underexposed and completely blank.

Moral: The spirit was willing but the flash was weak.

GIFTS

First girl: Weren't you kind of nervous when your boyfriend gave you all those beautiful gifts?

Second girl: No. I just kept calm and collected.

GLARE

Matt: Did you see that conductor? He glared at me as if I hadn't paid my fare.

Pat: And what did you do?

Matt: I glared right back as if I had.

GLASSES

The proprietor of a highly successful optical shop was instructing his son as to how to charge a customer.

"Son," he said, "after you have fitted the glasses, and he asks what the charge will be, you say, 'The charge is ten dollars.' Then pause and wait to see if he flinches.

"If the customer doesn't flinch, you then say, 'For the frames. The lenses will be another ten dollars.'

"Then you pause again, this time only slightly, and watch for the flinch. If the customer doesn't flinch this time, you say firmly, 'Each.'"

GOATS

Two goats in the desert found a tin can full of film. One of them nuzzled it until the lid came off. The film leader loosened around the spool, and the goat ate a few frames.

The second goat ate some, too. Soon they pulled all the film off the reel and consumed the whole of it.

When nothing was left but the can and the spool, the first goat said, "Wasn't that great?"

"Oh, I don't know," replied the second goat. "I thought the book was better."

GOLF

Golf is a lot of walking, broken up by disappointment and bad arithmetic.

෬─᎒─᎒෬

"You think so much of your old golf game you don't even remember when we were married."

"Of course I do, my dear; it was the day I sank that thirty-foot putt."

෬─᎒─᎒෬

A pastor and one of his parishioners were playing golf at a local country club. It was a very close match. At the last hole, the pastor teed up, addressed the ball, and swung his driver with great force. The ball stubbornly rolled off the tee and settled slowly some twelve feet away instead of sailing down the fairway.

The clergyman frowned, glared after the ball, and bit his lip, but said nothing.

His opponent regarded him for a moment and sighed, "Pastor, that is the most profane silence I have ever heard!"

∘𝕾—𝕮∘

"Reverend, I'm sorry I swore like that. That's what I like about you— when your golf ball goes into the rough, you don't swear."
"That may be—but where I spit, the grass dies!"

∘𝕾—𝕮∘

I shoot golf in the low seventies. When it gets any colder, I quit.

∘𝕾—𝕮∘

Wife: George, you promised you'd be home at 4:00. It's now 8:00.
George: Honey, please listen to me. Poor ol' Fred is dead. He just dropped over on the eighth green.
Wife: Oh, that's awful.
George: It surely was. For the rest of the game it was hit the ball, drag Fred, hit the ball, drag Fred.

∘𝕾—𝕮∘

Two men were beginning a game of golf. The first man stepped to the tee, and his first drive gave him a hole-in-one. The second man stepped up to the tee and said, "Okay, now I'll take my practice swing and then we'll start the game."

∘𝕾—𝕮∘

Bill: I'd move heaven and earth to break my 110 score.
Phil: Try moving heaven. You've already moved plenty of earth today.

∘𝕾—𝕮∘

Caddy: Let me say this about your game, mister. I wouldn't say you were the *worst* golfer I have ever seen on this course, but I've seen places today that I've never seen before.

∘𝕾—𝕮∘

"Look," the golfer screamed at his caddy, "if you don't keep your big mouth shut, you'll drive me out of my mind."

"That's no drive, mister," corrected the caddy. "That's a putt."

❦

Golfer: Notice any improvements since last year?
Caddy: Polished your clubs, didn't you?

Good

The man who says he is just as good as half the folks in the church seldom specifies which half.

Good News/Bad News

Doctor: I have some good news and some bad news.
Patient: What is the bad news?
Doctor: We had to cut off both of your legs.
Patient: What is the good news?
Doctor: There is a woman upstairs who would like to buy your shoes.

❦

Agent to writer: I've got some good news and some bad news.
Writer: First tell me the good news.
Agent: Paramount just loved your story, absolutely ate it up.
Writer: That's fantastic—and the bad news?
Agent: Paramount is my dog.

❦

The soldiers had been on the battlefield for weeks when the sergeant made an announcement.

"Men, I have some good news and some bad news for you. First the good news: Everyone will receive a change of socks. And now for the bad news. Walters, you will change with Hanson . . . Hanson you will change with Douglas . . . Douglas you will change with Kroeker . . . Kroeker you will change with Pedillia . . . Pedillia . . ."

GOOD OLD DAYS

Too many people keep looking back to the good old days:

1880 . . ."I walked fourteen miles through snow and rain to go to school."

1915 . . ."I had to walk five miles every day."

1936 . . ."It was eleven blocks to the bus stop every morning."

1950 . . ."I had to buy gasoline for my own car."

1966 . . ."When I drove to school as a boy, we didn't have power brakes, power steering, or power windows."

Our generation never got a break. When we were young they taught us to respect our elders. Now that we're older, they tell us to listen to the youth of the country.

Remember the good old days when the still, small voice within us used to be called conscience instead of a transistor radio?

The proud father brought home a backyard swing set for his children and immediately started to assemble it with all the neighborhood children anxiously waiting to play on it. After several hours of reading the directions, attempting to fit bolt A into slot B, etc., he finally gave up and called upon an old handyman working in a neighboring yard.

The old-timer came over, threw the directions away, and in a short while had the set completely assembled.

"It's beyond me," said the father, "how you got it together without even reading the instructions."

"To tell the truth," replied the old-timer, "I can't read, and when you can't read, you've got to think."

Good Samaritan

Sunday school teacher: In the story of the Good Samaritan, why did the Levite pass by on the other side?

Student: Because the poor man had already been robbed.

∽—∾

Sunday school teacher: Now class, you remember the story of the Good Samaritan. What would you do if you saw a man lying on the ground bleeding to death?

Little girl: I think I'd throw up.

Gotcha

A man sitting at his window one evening casually called to his wife: "There goes that woman Ken Roberts is in love with."

His wife in the kitchen dropped the plate she was drying, ran into the living room, knocked over a vase, and looked out the window. "Where, where?" she said.

"Over there," said the husband. "The woman in the blue dress standing on the corner."

"Why, you big idiot," she replied, "that's his wife."

"Yes, of course," answered the husband with a satisfied grin.

Government

It's becoming more and more difficult to support the government in the style to which it has become accustomed.

∽—∾

Hippie I: There is only one thing that bugs me about this revolution bit.

Hippie II: And what's that?

Hippie I: What happens to our unemployment checks when we overthrow the government?

∽—∾

The politician is my shepherd . . . I am in want;
He maketh me to lie down on park benches;
He leadeth me beside still factories;
He disturbeth my soul.
Yea, though I walk through the valley of the shadow of depression and recession,
I anticipate no recovery, for he is with me.
He prepareth a reduction in my salary in the presence of my enemies;
He anointeth my small income with great losses;
My expenses runneth over.
Surely unemployment and poverty shall follow me all the days of my life,
And I shall dwell in a mortgaged house forever.

Grocery Money

Husband: What have you been doing with all the grocery money I gave you?
Wife: Turn sideways and look in the mirror.

❧ H ❧

Haircut

Did you hear about the rock 'n' roll singer who wore a hearing aid for three years? Then he found out he only needed a haircut.

❦

A man entered a barbershop and said: "I am tired of looking like everyone else! I want a change! Part my hair from ear to ear!"

"Are you sure?"

"Yes!" said the man.

The barber did as he was told, and a satisfied customer left the shop.

Three hours passed and the man reentered the shop. "Put it back the way it was," he said.

"What's the matter?" said the barber. "Are you tired of being a nonconformist already?"

"No," he replied, "I'm tired of people whispering in my nose!"

❦

I couldn't stand my boy's long hair any longer, so I dragged him with me to the barbershop and ordered, "Give him a crew cut." The barber did just that and, so help me, I found I'd been bringing up somebody else's son!

Halt

A very new soldier was on sentry duty at the main gate of a military outpost. His orders were clear: No car was to enter unless it had a special sticker on the windshield. A big army car came up with a general seated in the back. The sentry said, "Halt, who goes there?"

The chauffeur, a corporal, said, "General Wheeler."

"I'm sorry, I can't let you through. You've got to have a sticker on the windshield."

The general said, "Drive on."

The sentry said, "Hold it. You really can't come through. I have orders to shoot if you try driving in without a sticker."

The general repeated, "I'm telling you, son, drive on."

The sentry walked up to the rear window and said, "General, I'm new at this: Do I shoot you or the driver?"

HANS SCHMIDT

A man was walking down the street and noticed a sign reading "Hans Schmidt's Chinese Laundry." Being of a curious nature, he entered and was greeted by an obviously Oriental man who identified himself as Hans Schmidt.

"How come you have a name like that?" inquired the stranger.

The Oriental explained in very broken English that when he landed in America he was standing in the immigration line behind a German. When asked his name, the German replied, "Hans Schmidt." When the immigration official asked the Oriental his name, he replied, "Sam Ting."

HAT

Husband: You call that a hat! My dear, I shall never stop laughing.
Wife: Oh, yes, you will. The bill will probably arrive tomorrow.

⌘

Husband: Where did you get that new hat?
Wife: Don't worry, dear. It didn't cost a thing. It was marked down from $20 to $10. So, I bought it with the $10 I saved.

⌘

First man: I felt sorry for your wife in church this morning when she had a terrible attack of coughing and everyone turned to look at her.

Second man: You don't need to worry about that. She was wearing a new spring hat and dress.

Heads or Tails

The soles of my shoes are so thin I can step on a dime and tell whether it's heads or tails.

Heaven and Hell

"There will be weeping, wailing, and gnashing of teeth among the wicked who pass on to the next world."
"What about those who haven't got any teeth?"
"Teeth will be provided."

∽⊝—⊝∾

An American tourist was looking down the crater of a large volcano in Greece and said, "It looks like hell."
The Greek guide responded, "You Americans have been everywhere."

∽⊝—⊝∾

"You're a minister, huh?"
"Yes, I am."
"What church?"
"Baptist."
"Oh, you're the narrow-minded bunch that believes only their group is going to make it to heaven."
"I'm even more narrow minded than that. I don't think all of *our* group are going to make it!"

Heavy, Heavy

Wife: Honey, will you still love me after I put on a few pounds?
Husband: Yes, I do.

∽⊝—⊝∾

She was so fat that she even had a shadow at high noon.

∽⊝—⊝∾

My girlfriend weighs five hundred pounds . . . she isn't fat but, boy, is she ever tall!

∽⊖—⊖∾

Wife to husband who just got off the pennyweight scale: "Your fortune says that you are handsome, debonair, and wealthy. It even has your weight wrong!"

∽⊖—⊖∾

I knew a guy in school who was so fat he sat in the first two rows!

∽⊖—⊖∾

She had mumps for five days and no one knew it.

∽⊖—⊖∾

She weighs one hundred and plenty.

∽⊖—⊖∾

She eats so much they use her picture on foodstamps.

∽⊖—⊖∾

If you really want to lose weight, there are only three things you must give up: breakfast, lunch, and dinner.

HELP! POLICE

Policeman: Name, please.
Motorist: Wilhelm von Corquerinski Popolavawitz.
Policeman: Well, don't let me catch you speeding again.

HENPECKED HUSBAND

A new group of male applicants had just arrived in heaven.

Peter looked them over and gave this order. "All men who were henpecked on earth, please step to the left; all those who were bosses in their own homes, step to the right."

The line quickly formed on the left. Only one man stepped to the right.

Peter looked at the frail little man standing by himself and inquired, "What makes you think you belong on that side?"

Without hesitation, the meek little man explained, "Because this is where my wife told me to stand."

⌁

"But, my dear," protested the henpecked husband, "I've done nothing. You've been talking for an hour and a half and I haven't said a word."

"I know," the wife replied. "But you listen like a wise-guy."

⌁

In my house, I make all the major decisions and my wife makes the minor ones. For example, I decide such things as East-West trade, crime in the streets, welfare cheating, and tax increases. My wife decides the minor things such as which house to buy, what kind of car we drive, how much money to spend, how to raise the children, etc.

⌁

A husband put in a flagstone walk from house to street. When he finished, he called his wife to come look. "It is terrible, the colors don't match, and the stones are crooked."

Weary and disappointed he asked, "How is it for length?"

High Heels

The invention of a girl who had been kissed on the forehead too many times.

Historical

"But, pastor," lamented the young husband in for counseling, "whenever Joan and I quarrel, she becomes historical."

"You mean, hysterical."

"No, historical. She is always digging up my past."

HIT-AND-RUN

When the traffic cop asked the prostrate man if he got the number of the hit-and-run driver, he said, "No, but I'd recognize my wife's laugh anywhere."

HITLER

Adolph Hitler was an avid believer in astrology and consulted with his special astrologer before making any decisions.

One day in consulting with him, Hitler asked, "On what day will I die?"

"You will die on a Jewish holiday," replied the astrologer.

"How can you be so sure of that?" asked Hitler.

"Any day you die will be a Jewish holiday," replied the astrologer.

∞⟶—⟵∞

At one point Hitler thought so much of himself that he ordered the government printing office to issue a stamp bearing his likeness. After a period of time the postal carriers began complaining that the stamps were falling off the envelopes. Every day their bags would be full of stamps.

Hitler paid a visit to the printers. He demanded to know why the highest grade of glue hadn't been used on his commemorative stamp.

"Oh, but it was," the trembling printer assured him. "We've looked into this unfortunate situation, and the problem, sir, is that the people are spitting on the wrong side."

HOMESICK

"I'm homesick! I'm homesick!"

"But you're at home!"

"I know—and I'm sick of it!"

Honorary Degree

An honorary degree is like the curl in the tail of a pig:
- It follows the main part of the animal.
- It is highly ornamental.
- In no way does it improve the quality of the ham.

Horse

If everyone owned a horse, this country would be more stabilized.

Hotels

Landlady: I charge $30.00 a night, and only $15.00 if you make your own bed.
Guest: I'll make my own bed.
Landlady: Hang on. I'll get you a hammer and nails.

◦⊖—⊖◦

My hotel room was so small the mice were hunchbacked.

Housekeeping

One thing I'll say for my wife, she's a very neat housekeeper. If I drop my socks on the floor, she picks them up. If I throw my clothes around, she hangs them up. I got up at three o'clock the other morning and went in the kitchen to get a glass of orange juice. I came back and found the bed made.

◦⊖—⊖◦

The United States is the only country where a housewife hires a woman to do her cleaning so she can do volunteer work at the day nursery where the cleaning woman leaves her child.

◦⊖—⊖◦

Nothing annoys a woman more than to have friends drop in unexpectedly and find the house looking as it usually does.

How Many Wheels?

Husband: That man is really stupid.
Wife: Why do you say that?
Husband: He thinks that a football coach has four wheels.
Wife: Isn't that silly! How many wheels does it have?

Huck

Finn and Huck were friends. Finn up and died. No one was worried, however. They said, "Huck'll bury Finn."

Humorist

A person who originates old jokes.

Hunch

Willy: I had a hunch today. I got up at seven, had seven dollars in my pocket, there were seven people at lunch, and there were seven horses in the race. I picked the seventh horse to win.
Billy: So he came in the winner?
Willy: No, he came in seventh.

Hunter

First hunter: How do you know you hit that duck?
Second hunter: Because I shot him in the foot and in the head at the same time.
First hunter: How could you possibly hit him in the foot and head at the same time?

Second hunter: He was scratching his head.

⁓◦—◦⁓

A hunter shot a duck and it fell into the lake. Quickly, he commanded his dog—a dog he had never worked before—to retrieve. The hound ran to the edge of the water, sniffed, and walked out on the lake. The hunter was amazed. He shot another duck; it, too, fell into the lake. Again the hound walked out on the water to retrieve the duck before it sank. At last, the hunter thought, he had something to show that friend of his who never let anything get to him. The next day the hunter suggested to his friend that they go do a little duck shooting. His friend shot a duck, and it fell into the lake. The dog walked across the water to retrieve it and dropped it at the shooter's feet.

The hunter asked his friend, "What do you think of my bird dog? Didn't you notice anything special about my dog?"

"I noticed one thing. He can't swim."

Husband and Wife

While reading the newspaper, Walter came across an article about a beautiful actress and model who married a boxer who was not noted for his IQ.

"I'll never understand," he said to his wife, "why the biggest jerks get the most attractive wives."

His wife replied, "Why, thank you, dear."

⁓◦—◦⁓

Husband: Ouch! I bumped my crazy bone.
Wife: Oh well, comb your hair right and the bump won't show.

⁓◦—◦⁓

Wife: I was a fool when I married you.
Husband: I don't doubt it, but I was much too infatuated to notice it.

⁓◦—◦⁓

Husband: Don't put that money in your mouth. There are germs on it.
Wife: Don't be silly. Even a germ can't live on the money you earn.

∾⊖—℮∾

Wife: Before we were married, we didn't sit this far apart in the car.
Husband: Well, dear, I didn't move.

∾⊖—℮∾

Gabby woman leaving party: There was something I wanted to say
before leaving, but I can't recall it just now.
Tired husband: Maybe it was good-bye.

∾⊖—℮∾

First husband: I think my wife is getting tired of me.
Second husband: What makes you feel that way?
First husband: She keeps wrapping my lunches in road maps.

∾⊖—℮∾

First man: Why do you wear dark glasses?
Second man: Because I can't bear to see my wife work so hard.

∾⊖—℮∾

Some people ask the secret of our long marriage. We take time to go
to a restaurant two times a week. A little candlelight, dinner, soft music,
and a slow walk home. She goes Tuesdays; I go Fridays.

∾⊖—℮∾

Husband: Where is yesterday's newspaper?
Wife: I wrapped the garbage in it.
Husband: Oh, I wanted to see it.

Wife: There wasn't much to see . . . just some orange peels and coffee grounds.

❧

A young man came home from the office and found his bride sobbing convulsively. "I feel terrible," she told me. "I was pressing your suit and I burned a big hole right in the seat of your trousers."

"Forget it," consoled her husband. "Remember that I've got an extra pair of pants for that suit."

"Yes, and it's lucky you have," said the little woman, drying her eyes. "I used them to patch the hole."

❧

Wife: You know the old saying, "What you don't know won't hurt you"?

Husband: What about it?

Wife: You must really be safe.

❧

A newly married couple was entertaining and among the guests was a man whose conduct was rather boisterous. At dinner he held up on his fork a piece of meat and in a vein of intended humor asked, "Is this pig?"

"To which end of the fork do you refer?" asked a quiet-looking man at the other end of the table.

❧

All husbands are alike, but they have different faces so that women can tell them apart.

❧

First wife: Does your husband lie awake all night?

Second wife: Yes, and he lies in his sleep, too.

❧

A lot of husbands have an impediment in their speech. Every time they open their mouths the wife interrupts.

⚬—⚬

Martha: Is your husband a bookworm?
Roberta: No, just an ordinary one.

⚬—⚬

Melba: My husband was named Man of the Year.
Pam: Well, that shows you what kind of year it's been.

Hymn

A song leader had a very rough time once when he was leading a choir and didn't pay attention to the words of the song. He said, "I want the women to sing the verse 'I will go home today,' and the men to come in on the chorus with 'Glad day, Glad day.'" The people were laughing too much to sing the song.

⚬—⚬

Three churches, all different denominations, were located on the same main intersection. One Sunday morning a passerby heard the first church singing, "Will There Be Any Stars in My Crown?"
The next church was singing, "No, Not One."
From the third church came, "Oh, That Will Be Glory For Me."

I Come Quickly

A new preacher had just begun his sermon. He was a little nervous and about ten minutes into the talk his mind went blank. He remembered to do what they had taught him in seminary when a situation like this arose—repeat your last point. Often this would help you remember what should come next. So he thought he would give it a try.

"Behold, I come quickly," he said. Still his mind was blank. He thought he would try it again. "Behold, I come quickly." Still nothing.

He tried it one more time with such force he fell forward, knocking the pulpit to one side, tripping over a flower pot, and falling into the lap of a little old lady in the front row.

The young preacher apologized and tried to explain what had happened. "That's all right, young man," said the little old lady. "It was my fault. I should have gotten out of the way. You told me three times you were coming!"

Ideal Husband

What Every Woman Expects:
He will be a brilliant conversationalist.
He will be very sensitive, kind, understanding, truly loving.
He will be a very hardworking man.
He will help around the house by washing dishes, vacuuming floors, and taking care of the yard.
He will help his wife raise the children.
He will be a man of emotional and physical strength.
He will be as smart as Einstein, but will look like Robert Redford.
What She Gets:
He always takes her to the best restaurants. (Someday he may even take her inside.)

He doesn't have any ulcers—he gives them.

Anytime he gets an idea in his head, he has the whole thing in a nutshell.

He's well-known as a miracle worker—it's a miracle when he works.

He supports his wife in the manner to which she was accustomed—he's letting her keep her job.

He's such a bore that he even bores you to death when he gives you a compliment.

He has occasional flashes of silence that make his conversation brilliant.

IDEAL WIFE

What every man expects his wife to be:

- Always beautiful and cheerful. Could have married movie stars but wanted only you.
- Hair that never needs curlers or beauty shops.
- Beauty that won't run in a rainstorm.
- Never sick, just allergic to jewelry and fur coats.
- Insists that moving the furniture by herself is good for her figure.
- Expert in cooking, cleaning house, fixing the car or TV, painting the house, and keeping quiet.
- Favorite hobbies: mowing the lawn and shoveling snow.
- Hates charge plates.
- Her favorite expression: "What can I do for you, dear?"
- Thinks you have Einstein's brain but look like Mr. America.
- Wishes you would go out with the boys so she could get some sewing done.
- Loves you because you're so-o-o sexy.

But actually:

- She speaks 140 words a minute with gusts up to 180.
- She once was a model for a totem pole.
- She's a light eater—as soon as it gets light she starts eating.
- Where there's smoke, there she is—cooking.
- If you get lost, open your wallet—she'll find you.

IMPRESSION

Next time you start to believe you are indispensable, stick your finger in a bowl of water. Now remove it. See the impression you've made?

INDIAN

There were three Indian squaws, one sitting on an elk hide, one on a deer hide, and one on a hippopotamus hide. The squaws on the elk and deer hides had one papoose each, while the squaw on the hippopotamus hide had two papooses.

Moral: The squaw on the hippopotamus equals the sum of the squaws on the other two hides.

∾⊖—⊖∾

Clerk: This jug was made by a real Indian.
Elmer: But it says here it's made in Cleveland, Ohio.
Clerk: Well, didn't you ever hear of the Cleveland Indians?

INFALLIBILITY

The pope would have never introduced papal infallibility if he had ever been married.

IN-LAWS

The extreme penalty for bigamy is two mothers-in-law.

∾⊖—⊖∾

"The man who married my mother got a prize."
"What was it?"

∾⊖—⊖∾

Wife: George! Come quickly! A wild tiger has just gone into mother's tent!

Husband: Well, he got himself into that mess; let him get out of it!

❦

"Was that your wife I saw you with last night?"

"No, that was my son-in-law, and I could cry every time I think about it."

Insane Asylum

A home for old joke-book writers.

❦

A policeman saw an old man pulling a box on a leash down a busy street. "Poor man," he thought. "I'd better humor him."

"That's a nice dog you've got there," he said to the old man.

"It isn't a dog, it's a box," said the man.

"Oh, I'm sorry," said the policeman. "I thought you were a bit simple-minded," and he walked on.

The old man turned and looked at the box. "We sure fooled him that time, Rover," he said.

❦

Late one night in the insane asylum one inmate shouted, "I am Napoleon."

Another said, "How do you know?"

The first inmate said, "God told me."

Just then, a voice from the next room shouted, "I did not."

Instructions

Pilot: Pilot to tower . . . pilot to tower . . . I am 300 miles from land and . . . 600 feet high and running out of gas . . . please instruct . . . over."

Tower: Tower to pilot . . . tower to pilot . . . repeat after me . . . Our Father, which art in heaven . . .

INSURANCE

To illustrate how swiftly life insurance claims are paid, one salesman said that his company's offices were on the tenth floor of a sixty-floor skyscraper, and that one day a man fell off the roof and was handed his check as he passed their floor.

◦∽─∾◦

The applicant for life insurance was finding it difficult to fill out the application. The salesman asked what the trouble was, and the man said that he couldn't answer the question about the cause of death of his father.

The salesman wanted to know why. After some embarrassment the client explained that his father had been hanged.

The salesman pondered for a moment. "Just write: 'Father was taking part in a public function when the platform gave way.'"

◦∽─∾◦

Bob: Does your uncle carry life insurance?
Paul: No, he just carries fire insurance. He knows where he is going.

INTERVIEW

"Now this is the verbal part of your employment test. What does Aurora Borealis mean?"

"It means I don't get the job!"

◦∽─∾◦

"Were you hired by the radio station?"

"N-n-no, they s-s-aid I w-w-wasn't t-t-tall enough!"

INTRODUCTION

Introducing a speaker: There isn't anything that I wouldn't do for Mr. _____, and there isn't anything he wouldn't do for me. That's why we have gone through life not doing anything for each other.

∽⊝—⊝∾

Speaker: After an introduction like that, I can hardly wait to hear what I am going to say myself.

∽⊝—⊝∾

In his last appearance, he drew a line three blocks long. Then they took his chalk away.

∽⊝—⊝∾

You have heard it said before that this speaker needs no introduction. Well, I have heard him and he needs all the introduction he can get.

∽⊝—⊝∾

You haven't heard nothing until you've heard our speaker of the evening. Then you've heard nothing.

INVALID

Christy: I was an invalid once.
Lisa: You were? When was that?
Christy: When I was a baby I couldn't walk until I was a year old.

Inventor

Needless to say, one of the most successful inventors of all time was the man who invented a hay-baling machine. He made a bundle.

∾⊖⊖∾

The next most successful man was the chemist who created a lubricant for furniture wheels. He called it castor oil.

∾⊖⊖∾

"I have a friend who is a real inventor. He took the fender from a Chevy, a motor from a Ford, and the transmission from a Sting Ray."
"Well, what did he get?"
"Three years."

IRS

Q: What do you need when you have an IRS auditor buried to his neck in concrete?
A: More concrete.

∾⊖⊖∾

Don't be surprised if your next income tax form is simplified to contain only four lines:

1. What was your income last year?
2. What were your expenses?
3. How much do you have left?
4. Send it in.

∾⊖⊖∾

The three R's of the IRS: This is ours, that is ours, everything is ours.

∾⊖⊖∾

Someday the income tax return will be simplified to: How much money have you got? Where is it? When can you get it?

⌾—⌾

First friend: Two things we're sure of—death and taxes.
Second friend: Yeah, but one thing about death, it doesn't get worse every time Congress meets.

⌾—⌾

IRS agent to taxpayer: I'm afraid we can't allow you to deduct last year's tax as a bad investment.

⌾—⌾

"What kind of work do you do?"
"I work for the Bureau of Internal Revenue."
"Doesn't everybody?"

Isms

Communism: If you have two cows, you give both cows to the government, and then the government sells you some of the milk.
Socialism: If you have two cows, you give both cows to the government, and then the government gives you some of the milk.
Naziism: If you have two cows, the government shoots you and takes both cows.
Facism: If you have two cows, you milk both of them and give the government half of the milk.
New Dealism: If you have two cows, you kill one, milk the other and pour the milk down the drain.
Capitalism: If you have two cows, you sell one cow and buy a bull.

It's All in the Family

Advice to mothers: Unless you deliberately set aside a little time for regular relaxation, you will not be able to efficiently care for your family. Therefore, plan to relax a minimum of an hour and a half every fifteen years.

⚬―⚬

After dinner, members of a lot of families suffer from dish-temper.

⚬―⚬

Dan: What does your mother do for a headache?
Stan: She sends me out to play.

⚬―⚬

Father: Did you reprimand Walter for mimicking me?
Mother: Yes, I told him not to act like a fool.

⚬―⚬

A Kansas cyclone hit a farmhouse just before dawn one morning. It lifted the roof off, picked up the beds on which the farmer and his wife slept, and set them down gently in the next county.

The wife began to cry.

"Don't be scared, Mary," her husband said. "We're not hurt."

Mary continued to cry. "I'm not scared," she responded between sobs. "I'm sorry 'cause this is the first time in fourteen years we've been out together."

⚬―⚬

Son: Dad, what is "creeping inflation"?
Father: It's when your mother starts out asking for new shoes and ends up with a complete new outfit.

⚬―⚬

Son: Dad, what is a weapon?
Father: Why, son, that's something you fight with.
Son: Is mother your weapon?

⚬―⚬

Little boy to departing relative, "There's no hurry, Auntie. Daddy has put the clock a whole hour ahead."

∾⊙—↶

My brother was sort of odd. I remember once on his birthday he fell down a dry well, so we lowered his birthday cake to him. He didn't even tug on the rope to say thanks.

IT'S THE PLUMBER

Once upon a time there was a parrot who could say only three little words: "Who is it?" One day when the parrot was alone in the house, there was a loud knock on the door. "Who is it?" screeched the parrot.

"It's the plumber," the visitor responded.

"Who is it?" repeated the parrot.

"It's the plumber, I tell you," was the reply. "You called me to tell me your cellar was flooded."

Again the parrot called, "Who is it?"

By this time, the plumber became so angry that he fainted. A neighbor rushed over to see the cause of the commotion and found the visitor had died because of a heart attack. He looked at the man and said, "Who is it?"

The parrot answered, "It's the plumber!"

⊰ J ⊱

JELLO

He's a regular Rock of Jell-O.

JOB

Q: Why was Job always cold in bed?
A: Because he had such miserable comforters.

⌁

"Did you know that Job spoke when he was a very small baby?"
"Where does it say that?"
"It says, 'Job cursed the day he was born.'"

JOKES

Dan: How do you like my jokes?
Stan: I can't see anything funny in them.
Dan: Oh well, you'll probably catch on after a while and laugh.
Stan: No, I laughed at them twenty years ago.

⌁

Gary: So you didn't like my jokes.
Harry: No, they were terrible.
Gary: Oh, I don't know about that—I threw a bunch of them in the furnace and the fire roared.

JUDGE

Judge: Thirty years in prison!
Prisoner: But, Judge, I won't live that long!

Judge: Don't worry, do what you can.

∽⊙—⊙∽

Judge: I've decided to give you a suspended sentence.
Prisoner: Thank you, Your Honor.
Judge: For what? You're going to be hanged.

JUMPING TO CONCLUSIONS

Jumping to conclusions is not half as much exercise as digging for facts.

❧ K ❧

Kayak

Did you hear about the Eskimo who had put some oil heaters in his kayak and was surprised when they exploded and set fire to it? Which only goes to prove that you can't have your kayak and heat it, too.

Kids

Children would all be brought up perfectly if families would just swap kids. Everyone knows what ought to be done with the neighbor's kids.

❧—⊙—❧

"Young man, there were two cookies in the pantry this morning. May I ask how it happens that there is only one now?"
"Must have been so dark I didn't see the other one."

❧—⊙—❧

Little Jane, whose grandmother was visiting her family, was going to bed when her mother called:
"Don't forget, dear, to include Grandma in your prayers tonight, that God should bless her and let her live to be very, very old."
"Oh, she's old enough," replied Jane. "I'd rather pray that God would make her young."

❧—⊙—❧

My son is such an introvert he can't even lead in silent prayer.

❧—⊙—❧

Mother: How could you be so rude as to tell your sister she's stupid? Tell her you're sorry.
Boy: Sis, I'm sorry you're stupid.

<hr/>

Little Mary, the daughter of a radio announcer, was invited to a friend's house for dinner. The hostess asked if Mary would honor them by saying grace.

Delighted, the little girl cleared her throat, looked at her wristwatch and said, "This food, friends, is coming to you through the courtesy of Almighty God!"

<hr/>

Mother: Aunt Matilda won't kiss you with that dirty face.
Boy: That's what I figured.

<hr/>

A hungry little boy was beginning to eat his dinner when his father reminded him that they hadn't prayed.

"We don't have to," said the little boy. "Mommy is a good cook!"

<hr/>

Joe: When I would wear my hand-me-downs to school, all the boys would make fun of me.
Moe: What did you do?
Joe: I hit them over the head with my purse!

<hr/>

Johnny: Will I get everything I pray for, Mama?
Mother: Everything that's good for you, dear.
Johnny: Oh, what's the use, then? I get that anyway.

<hr/>

Mother: Why did you put this live frog in your sister's bed?
Bob: Because I couldn't find a dead mouse.

∾ᴑ—ᴇ∾

A father, whose looks are not such as to warrant the breaking up of all existing statues of Apollo, tells this on himself:

My little girl was sitting on my lap facing a mirror. After gazing intently at her reflection for some minutes, she said, "Daddy, did God make you?"

"Certainly, my dear," I told her.

"And did he make me, too?" taking another look in the mirror.

"Certainly, dear. What makes you ask?"

"Seems to me He's doing better work lately."

∾ᴑ—ᴇ∾

Father: Son, do you realize when Lincoln was your age he was already studying hard to be a lawyer?

Son: Right, Pop, and when he was your age, he was already President of the United States!

∾ᴑ—ᴇ∾

Bobby had been to a birthday party, and, knowing his weakness, his mother looked him straight in the eye and said, "I hope you didn't ask for a second piece of cake."

"No," replied Bobby. "I only asked Mrs. Jones for the recipe so you could make some like it and she gave me two more pieces just of her own accord."

∾ᴑ—ᴇ∾

One nice thing about kids is that they don't keep telling you boring stories about the clever things their parents said.

∾ᴑ—ᴇ∾

My children are at the perfect age . . . too old to cry at night and too young to borrow my car.

∽⊙―⊙∾

Little girl: Grandfather, make like a frog.
Grandfather: What do you mean, make like a frog?
Little girl: Mommy says we're going to make a lot of money when you croak!

KING

The lion went up to the rhinoceros and asked, "Who is the king of the jungle?"

"You are, O lion," came the answer.

The lion went up to the hippopotamus and asked, "Who is the king of the jungle?"

The hippo said, "You are, O lion."

The lion went up to the elephant and asked, "Who is the king of the jungle?"

For an answer the elephant seized the lion with his trunk, threw him high in the air, caught him on the way down, and slammed him hard against a tree.

The lion arose, half-dazed, shook himself, and said weakly, "Just because you don't know the right answer, you don't have to get sore."

KING HEROD

During a seminary class, the lesson centered on the problem of King Herod offering up half his kingdom to see the daughter of Herodias dance.

"Now, what if you had this problem and you made the offer of anything she wanted and the girl came to you asking for the head of John the Baptist, and you didn't want to give her the head of John. What would you do?" asked the professor.

Soon a hand was raised. "I'd tell her," said one student, "that the head of John the Baptist was not in the half of the kingdom I was offering to her."

Kiss

Girl: I'm sorry but I don't kiss on the first date.
Boy: How about on the last one?

❦

Husband: I'd like to know whatever became of the old-fashioned girls who fainted when a man kissed them.
Wife: What I'd like to know is what happened to the old-fashioned men who made them faint.

❦

Boy: I want to be honest. You're not the first girl I've kissed.
Girl: I want to be honest. You've got a lot to learn.

Knock, Knock

"Knock, knock."
"Who's there?"
"Wendy."
"Wendy who?"
"Wendy red red robin comes bob bob bobbin' along . . ."

❦

"Knock, knock."
"Who's there?"

"Tarzan."
"Tarzan who?"
"Tarzan stripes forever."

❦

"Knock, knock."
"Who's there?"
"Divan."
"Divan who?"
"Divan the bathtub—I'm drowning."

❦

"Knock, knock."
"Who's there?"
"Oswald."
"Oswald who?"
"Oswald mah gum."

❦

"Knock, knock."
"Who's there?"
"Honeydew and cantaloupe."
"Honeydew and cantaloupe who?"
"Honeydew you love me? We cantaloupe now."

❦

"Knock, knock."
"Who's there?"
"Freeze."
"Freeze who?"
"Freeze a jolly good fellow."

❦

"Knock, knock."
"Who's there?"

"Olive."
"Olive who?"
"Olive you."

Knowledge

He who knows but little shares it often.

⁋ L ⁋

LADY-KILLER

Guy: I'm a lady-killer.
Gal: Yeah, they take one look at you and drop dead.

LAMPPOST

First Russian: In America the people are so honest, you can hang your watch on a lamppost and come back in three weeks and it's still there.

Second Russian: You mean to say that in America you can hang your watch on a lamppost and come back in three weeks and your watch is still there?

First Russian: No, the lamppost is still there.

LANGUAGE

Q: What's more clever than speaking in several languages?
A: Keeping your mouth shut in one.

LARGE

"When I got on the bus three men got up to give me their seats."
"Did you take them?"

LARK

Joe: I spent ten dollars on a canary yesterday.
Moe: That's nothing. I spent fifty on a lark.

LATE

Every day Mr. Smith's secretary was twenty minutes late. Then one day she slid snugly into place only five minutes tardy.

"Well," said Mr. Smith, "this is the earliest you've ever been late."

∽≎⌒∾

Husband: I have tickets for the theater.
Wife: Wonderful, darling. I'll start dressing right away.
Husband: That's a good idea. The tickets are for tomorrow night.

LAUGH

"Did you see that young lady smile at me?"
"That's nothing. The first time I saw you, I laughed right out loud."

∽≎⌒∾

From the moment I picked up your joke book until I laid it down I was convulsed with laughter. Some day I intend to read it.

LAW

Judge: What terrible crime has this man committed?
Lawyer: He has not done anything wrong. He was merely an innocent bystander when the killer shot a clerk in a hold-up. We are holding him as a witness.
Judge: And where is the killer?
Lawyer: He's out on bail.

∽≎⌒∾

Son: Papa! Papa! The lid to our coal-shoot was left open and a man fell down inside. What should I do?
Father: Quick! Put the cover on it. I'll call a cop and have him arrested before he can sue us.

∽≎⌒∾

A man arrested for gambling came before the judge. "We weren't playing for money," he explained to the judge. "We were just playing for chips."

"Chips are just the same as money," the judge sternly replied. "I fine you fifteen dollars."

The defendant looked sad, then slowly reached into his pocket and handed the judge three blue chips.

LAWYER

Witness: Well, I think—
Lawyer: Don't think! In this courtroom you are to tell what you know, not what you think!
Witness: Well, I'm not a lawyer. I can't talk without thinking!

❧——❧

"And what do you do, sir?"
"I'm a criminal lawyer."
"Aren't they all!"

❧——❧

Did you hear that my lawyer was in an accident? The ambulance backed up without warning.

❧——❧

Do you know the difference between a dead chicken in the road and a dead lawyer in the road? There are skid marks in front of the chicken.

❧——❧

Do you know why they bury lawyers sixteen feet deep in the ground? Because lawyers are real good down deep.

❧——❧

Did you hear about the man who was walking through a graveyard and noticed a gravestone that said, "Here lies a lawyer and good man."

"Imagine that," said the man to himself, "two men buried in the same grave."

※ ⊙ ⊙ ※

Did you hear the good news and the bad news? The good news is that a busload of lawyers just ran off the cliff. The bad news is that there were three empty seats on the bus.

※ ⊙ ⊙ ※

"What do you have when you have 20,000 lawyers at the bottom of the ocean?"
"You have a good start."

※ ⊙ ⊙ ※

Lawyers can compress the most words into the smallest ideas better than anyone I have ever met.

※ ⊙ ⊙ ※

Brenda: My dad wanted to be a lawyer badly.
Sharon: Is there any other kind of lawyers except bad ones?

※ ⊙ ⊙ ※

On visiting a seriously ill lawyer in the hospital, his friend found him sitting up in bed, frantically leafing through the Bible.
"What are you doing?" asked the friend.
"Looking for loopholes," replied the lawyer.

※ ⊙ ⊙ ※

Judge: Guilty or not guilty?
Prisoner: Well, I thought I was guilty, but I've been talking to my lawyer and he's convinced me I'm not guilty.

※ ⊙ ⊙ ※

A lawyer had successfully handled a difficult law case for a wealthy friend. Following the happy outcome of the case, the friend and client called on the lawyer, expressed his appreciation of his work, and handed him a handsome Moroccan leather wallet.

The lawyer looked at the wallet in astonishment and handed it back with a sharp reminder that a wallet could not possibly compensate him for his services. "My fee for that work," acidly snapped the attorney, "is five hundred dollars."

The client opened the wallet, removed a one-thousand dollar bill, replaced it with a five-hundred dollar bill, and handed it back to the lawyer with a smile.

❧

Crook: I got nearly a million in cash in my bank box. Can you get me off?

Lawyer: Believe me, pal, you'll never go to prison with that kind of money.

And sure enough, he did not. He went to prison flat broke.

LAZY

My friend, have you heard of the town of Yawn, on the banks of the river Slow, where blooms the Waitawhile flower fair, where the Sometimeorother scents the air, and the Softgoeasys grow?

It lies in the valley of Whatstheuse, in the province of Letherslide; that tired feeling is native there—it's the home of the listless Idon'tcare, where the Putitoffs abide.

❧

Mike: I always do my hardest work before breakfast.
Sandy: What's that?
Mike: Getting up.

LECTURE

At a lecture series a very poor speaker was on the platform. As he was speaking, people in the audience began to get up and leave. After about ten minutes there was only one man left. Finally the man stopped speaking and asked the man why he remained to the end. "I'm the next speaker," was the reply.

❦

A lecturer announced to his audience that the world would probably end in seven billion years.

"How long did you say?" came a terrified voice from the rear.

"Seven billion years."

"Thank goodness!" said the voice. "I thought for a moment you had said seven million."

❦

Interrupted by the sound of the bell announcing the end of the class, the professor was annoyed to see the students noisily preparing to leave even though he was in the middle of his lecture. "Just a moment, class," he said, "I have a few more pearls to cast."

LIAR

The game warden was walking through the mountains when he encountered a hunter with a gun. "This is a good territory for hunting, don't you think?" suggested the warden.

"You bet it is," said the hunter enthusiastically. "I killed one of the finest bucks yesterday—it weighed at least two hundred fifty pounds."

"Deer are out of season now," said the warden. "Do you know that you are talking to a game warden?"

"No, I was not aware of that," said the hunter. "And I'll bet you didn't know that you've been talking to the biggest liar in the state."

❦

A minister wound up the services one morning by saying, "Next Sunday I am going to preach on the subject of liars. And in this connection, as a preparation for my discourse, I should like you all to read the seventeenth chapter of Mark."

On the following Sunday, the preacher rose to begin and said, "Now, then, all of you who have done as I requested and read the seventeenth chapter of Mark, please raise your hands."

Nearly every hand in the congregation went up. Then said the preacher, "You are the people I want to talk to. There is no seventeenth chapter of Mark!"

LIES

The following will help you to identify lies that are often told:

- I'm only thinking of you, dear. Meaning: I am now about to get a bit of my own back.
- I don't want to make you unhappy. Meaning: I will now repeat to you certain malicious gossip which will reduce you to sleepless misery.
- I'm bound to admit. Meaning: I will now confuse the main issue.
- I'm not one to criticize. Meaning: I shall now proceed to find fault with all you have done.
- I'm as broad-minded as anyone. Meaning: All my ideas on this subject are hopelessly out-of-date.
- I hope I know my place. Meaning: I am about to step right out of it and tell you a few home truths.
- I'm a tolerant sort of fellow. Meaning: I can't endure you for another moment and am now preparing to throw you out of the house.

LIGHTWEIGHTS

If it wasn't for her Adam's apple, she wouldn't have any shape at all.

∞⊖—⊖∞

He was so thin he had to wear skis in the bathtub to keep from going down the drain.

∞⊖—⊖∞

When her husband takes her to a restaurant, the headwaiter asks him to check his umbrella.

❦

She was so thin that when she turned sideways and stuck out her tongue she looked like a zipper.

❦

She has to run around in the shower to get wet.

LOAN

Stan: How about lending me fifty dollars?

Dan: Sorry, I can only let you have twenty-five dollars.

Stan: But why not the entire fifty dollars, Dan?

Dan: No, twenty-five dollars only. That way it's even—each one of us loses twenty-five dollars.

❦

"Hello, this is George."

"Hello, George. What's on your mind?"

"I'm broke down in Los Angeles and I need two hundred dollars right away."

"There must be something wrong with the line. I can't hear you."

"I say, I want to borrow two hundred dollars."

"I can't hear a word you're saying."

Operator (coming on the line): "Hello! This is the operator. I can hear your party very plainly."

"Then you give him the two hundred dollars."

❦

A man came into the bank to get a loan. He went up to the teller and said, "Who arranges for loans?"

"I'm sorry, sir," the teller told him, "but the loan arranger is out to lunch."

"All right," said the man. "May I speak to Tonto?"

∽⊖—⊖∾

Larry: Lend me ten dollars.

Harry: I can't spare it.

Larry: All right, lend me ten dollars and give me five dollars now. Then I'll owe you five dollars and you'll owe me five dollars, and we'll call it square.

∽⊖—⊖∾

"Have you money for a cup of coffee, mister?"

"No, but don't worry about me, I'll get along all right."

∽⊖—⊖∾

"Say, mister, would you give me a quarter for a sandwich?"

"I dunno. Lemme see the sandwich!"

∽⊖—⊖∾

Credit manager: Do you have any money in the bank?

Loan applicant: Certainly.

Credit manager: How much?

Loan applicant: I don't know. I haven't shaken it lately.

∽⊖—⊖∾

Beggar: Sir, could you spare twenty dollars?

Man: Twenty dollars! What makes you think you can ask people for money like that?

Beggar: I just thought that it would be best to put all my begs in one ask it.

∽⊖—⊖∾

Creditors have better memories than debtors.

∽⊖—⊖∾

Q: Where do shellfish go to borrow money?
A: To the prawnbroker.

❧ ❧

"Dear Dad: Let me hear from you more often, even if it's only five or ten."

❧ ❧

"Loan me ten dollars, will you?"
"No."
"I was only fooling."
"I wasn't."

❧ ❧

"What a lot of friends we lose through their borrowing money from us."
"Yes, it is touch and go with most of them."

❧ ❧

Lady: Young man, I am going to give a quarter not because you deserve it, but because it pleases me to do so.
Beggar: Thanks, but why not make it a dollar so you can really enjoy yourself?

Lord's Prayer

Children's versions of the Lord's Prayer:
Our Father, Who art in heaven, hello! What be Thy name?
Give us this day our daily breath.
Our Father, Who art in heaven, Hollywood be Thy name.
Our Father, Who art in heaven, Harold be Thy name.
Give us this day our jelly bread.
Lead us not into creation.
Deliver us from weevils.
Deliver us from eagles.

❧ ❧

Two lawyers were bosom friends. Much to the amazement of one, the other became a Sunday school teacher. "I bet you don't even know the Lord's Prayer," he fumed.

"Everybody knows that," the other replied. "It's 'Now I lay me down to sleep—'"

"You win," said the other admiringly. "I didn't know you knew so much about the Bible."

LOVE

A little foolishness and a lot of curiosity.

∾⊖—⊖∾

Love is blind—and marriage is an eye-opener.

∾⊖—⊖∾

Guy: Margie, I love you! I love you, Margie!
Gal: In the first place, you don't love me; and in the second place, my name isn't Margie.

∾⊖—⊖∾

Becky: Do you love me with all your heart and soul?
Dave: Uh-huh.
Becky: Do you think I'm the most beautiful girl in the world?
Dave: Uh-huh.
Becky: Do you think my lips are like rose petals?
Dave: Uh-huh.
Becky: Oh, you say the most beautiful things.

∾⊖—⊖∾

Better to have loved a short man than never to have loved a tall.

LUNATICS

Son: How do they catch lunatics, Dad?
Dad: With lipstick, beautiful dresses, and pretty smiles.

⊰ M ⊱

Mad

Ralph: The police shot my dog.
Gary: Was he mad?
Ralph: Well, he wasn't too pleased about it.

Maid

Wife: I've been asked for a reference for our last maid. I've said she's lazy, unpunctual, and impertinent. How can I add anything in her favor?
Husband: You might say that she's got a good appetite and sleeps well.

Marblehead

"In Massachusetts they named a town after you."
"What is it?"
"Marblehead."

Mark Twain

Mark Twain was once trapped by a bore who lectured to him about the hereafter: "Do you realize that every time I exhale, some poor soul leaves this world and passes on to the great beyond?"
"Really? Why don't you try chewing cloves?"

⌁

Mark Twain's hostess at the opera had chattered so much that no one in her box had been able to enjoy the singing. At the end of the performance she said, "Mr. Clemens, I want you to be my guest next Friday night, too. They are going to give Tosca then."

"Charmed," said Twain. "I've never heard you in that."

◦❧—❧◦

Mark Twain once encountered a friend at the races who said, "I'm broke. I wish you'd buy me a ticket back to town."

Twain said, "Well, I'm pretty broke myself but I'll tell you what to do. You hide under my seat and I'll cover you with my legs." It was agreed and Twain then went to the ticket office and bought two tickets. When the train was underway and the supposed stowaway was snug under the seat, the conductor came by and Twain gave him the two tickets.

"Where is the other passenger?" asked the conductor.

Twain tapped on his forehead and said in a loud voice, "That is my friend's ticket. He is a little eccentric and likes to ride under the seat."

MAROONED

"I had a terrible dream. I dreamed I was marooned on an island with twelve beautiful women."

"What's wrong with that?"

"Did you ever try and cook and wash for twelve women?"

MARRIAGE

Keep your eyes wide open before marriage—half-shut afterward.

◦❧—❧◦

Marriage is like the army . . . everyone complains, but you'd be surprised at how many reenlist.

◦❧—❧◦

Son: How much does it cost to get married, Dad?
Dad: I don't know. I'm still paying on it.

◦◦—◦◦

"Can you take dictation?"
"No, I've never been married."

◦◦—◦◦

She calls her husband "Henry." He's the eighth.

◦◦—◦◦

Jay: I have half a mind to get married.
Bufe: That's all you need.

◦◦—◦◦

"And at her request you gave up drinking?"
"Yes."
"And you stopped smoking for the same reason?"
"I did."
"And it was for her that you gave up dancing, card playing, and billiards?"
"Absolutely."
"Then, why didn't you marry her?"
"Well, after all this reforming I realized I could do better."

◦◦—◦◦

First girl: My pastor said we could have sixteen husbands.
Second girl: Are you sure about that?
First girl: Why, yes. At the last wedding at the church I heard him say, "Four better, four worse, four richer, and four poorer!"

◦◦—◦◦

Marriage is like a railroad sign—you see a girl and stop. Then you look. And after you're married you listen.

❧───❧

Husband: Why do you weep and snuffle over a TV program and the imaginary woes of people you have never met?
Wife: For the same reason you scream and yell when a man you don't know makes a touchdown.

❧───❧

Wife: I read about a man who speaks eight languages who married a woman who speaks two.
Husband: That seems to be about the right handicap.

❧───❧

The most dangerous year in married life is the first. Then follows the second, third, fourth, fifth . . .

❧───❧

Marriage is like horseradish—men praise it with tears in their eyes.

❧───❧

"Now that looks like a happily married couple."
"Don't be too sure, my dear. They're probably saying the same thing about us."

❧───❧

Marriage is like a violin—after the music stops, the strings are still attached.

❧───❧

Wife: At least you could talk to me while I sew.
Husband: Why don't you sew to me while I read?

∽☉—☉∾

Wife: If you had to do it over again, would you marry me, dear?
Husband: Of course, if I had to do it over again.

∽☉—☉∾

A couple's happy married life almost went on the rocks because of the presence in the household of old Aunt Emma. For seven long years she lived with them, always crotchety, always demanding. Finally the old girl died.

On the way back from the cemetery, the husband confessed to his wife, "Darling, if I didn't love you so much, I don't think I would have put up with having your Aunt Emma in the house all those years."

His wife looked at him, aghast. "My Aunt Emma!" she cried. "I thought she was your Aunt Emma!"

∽☉—☉∾

One night a wife found her husband standing over their baby's crib. Silently she watched him. As he stood looking down at the sleeping infant, she saw on his face a mixture of emotions: disbelief, doubt, delight, amazement, enchantment, skepticism.

Touched by this unusual display and the deep emotions it aroused, with eyes glistening she slipped her arm around her husband.

"A penny for your thoughts," she said.

"It's amazing!" he replied. "I just can't see how anybody can make a crib like that for only $46.50."

∽☉—☉∾

Tom: If a wedding means showers for the bride, what does it mean for the groom?
Jerry: Curtains.

∽☉—☉∾

A knock came at the door. "Who is it?" asked the wife.
A gruff voice replied, "It's Jack the Ripper."
She turned to her husband and said, "It's for you, dear."

◦◦—◦◦

My wife puts so much grease on her face at night you'd think she was going to swim the English Channel.

◦◦—◦◦

A wife sought the advice of a fortune-teller, who said, "Prepare yourself for widowhood. Your husband is going to die a violent death."
The wife sighed deeply and asked, "Will I be acquitted?"

◦◦—◦◦

A woman offered a brand-new Porsche for sale for a price of ten dollars. A man answered the ad, but he was slightly disbelieving.
"What's the gimmick?" he inquired.
"No gimmick," the woman answered. "My husband died, and in his will he asked that the car be sold and the money given to his secretary."

◦◦—◦◦

"I understand the government is going to handle marriages."
"Yes."
"I wonder what department they'll be in?"
"I think it will be the War Department."

◦◦—◦◦

Wife: I can't sleep, dear. I keep thinking there's a mouse under the bed.
Husband: Well, start thinking there's a cat under the bed and go to sleep.

Marriage Counselor

Marriage counselor: Do you enjoy talking to each other?
Counselee: Oh, we enjoy talking to each other all right. The problem is listening to each other.

⌁—⌀—⌁

Marriage counselor: Do you encourage your husband in his work?
Counselee: I do my best. I keep telling him he ought to ask for a raise.

Marshmallow

Last night I dreamed I ate a five-pound marshmallow. When I woke up, my pillow was gone.

Match

Writer: Can't you suggest something to put a finishing touch on my story?
Editor: Yes. A match.

Mechanic

Motorist: What will it cost to fix my car?
Mechanic: What's wrong with it?
Motorist: I don't know.
Mechanic: $79.95!

Medicare

A sample of what might happen if we had socialized medicine is currently making the rounds. It goes something like this:

A man feeling the need of medical care went to the medical building for that purpose, and upon entering the front door found himself faced with a battery of doors, each marked with the names of ailments such as appendicitis, heart, cancer, etc.

He felt sure his trouble could be diagnosed as appendicitis, so he entered the door so marked. Upon entering, he found himself faced with two more doors, one marked male and the other female. He entered the door marked male and found himself in another corridor where there were two doors, one marked Protestant and the other Catholic.

Since he was a Protestant, he entered the proper door and found himself facing two more doors, one marked taxpayer and the other marked nontaxpayer. He still owned equity in his home, so he went through the door marked taxpayer, and found himself confronted with two more doors marked single and married.

He had a wife at home, so he entered the proper door and once more there were two more doors, marked Republican and the other Democrat.

SINCE HE WAS A REPUBLICAN HE ENTERED THE DOOR AND FELL NINE FLOORS TO THE ALLEY.

MEDICINE

The doctor told me to take this medicine after a hot bath. I could hardly finish drinking the bath!

∽<del>୨</del>—<del>ଜ</del>∾

Doctor: Are you still taking the cough medicine I gave you?
Patient: No, I tasted it and decided I'd rather have the cough.

∽<del>୨</del>—<del>ଜ</del>∾

Did you hear about the doctor who wrote out a prescription in the usual doctor's fashion? The patient used it for two years as a railroad pass. Twice it got him into Radio City Music Hall, and once into Yankee Stadium. It came in handy as a letter from his employer to the cashier to increase his salary. And as a climax, his daughter played it on the piano and won a scholarship to the Curtis Music Conservatory.

MELODY IN F
(THE PRODIGAL SON)

Feeling footloose and frisky, a feather-brained fellow
Forced his fond father to fork over the farthings,
And flew far to foreign fields
And fabulously frittered his fortune with faithless friends.
Fleeced by his fellows in folly, and facing famine,
He found himself a feed-flinger in a filthy farmyard.
Fairly famishing, he fain would've filled his frame
With foraged food from fodder fragments.
"Fooey, my father's flunkies fare far finer,"
The frazzled fugitive forlornly fumbled, frankly facing facts.
Frustrated by failure, and filled with foreboding,
He fled forthwith to his family.
Falling at his father's feet, he forlornly fumbled, "Father, I've flunked,
And fruitlessly forfeited family fellowship favor."
The far-sighted father, forestalling further flinching,
Frantically flagged the flunkies.
"Fetch a fatling from the flock and fix a feast."
The fugitive's fault-finding brother frowned
On fickle forgiveness of former folderol.
But the faithful father figured,
"Filial fidelity is fine, but the fugitive is found!
What forbids fervent festivity?
Let flags be unfurled! Let fanfares flare!"
Father's forgiveness formed the foundation
For the former fugitive's future fortitude!

MEMOIRS

There's nothing a man can do to improve himself so much as writing his memoirs.

MEMORY VERSE

A little boy was writing the memory verse for the day on the blackboard: "Do one to others as others do one to you."

Sunday school teacher: Do you remember your memory verse?
Student: I sure do. I even remember the zip code . . . John 3:16.

MEN

Wife: All men are fools.
Husband: Of course, dear. We are made like that so you girls won't have to be old maids.

MENTAL BLOCK

A street on which several psychiatrists live.

MESS

College boy to his mother: "I decided that I want to be a political science major and clean up the mess in the world!"

"That's very nice," purred his mother. "You can go upstairs and start with your room."

⤲ ⤲

First husband: Does your wife keep a messy home?
Second husband: Let's put it this way—when the toast pops out of the toaster, it takes an hour to find it.

METAL AGE

We live in the Metal Age:

- silver in the hair.
- gold in the teeth.
- lead in the pants.
- iron in the veins.

METRIC COOKIE

A gram cracker.

MIDDLE AGE

Middle age is when all one's energy goes to waist.

∽⊙–⊘∾

You're middle-aged when your stomach goes out for a career of its own.

∽⊙–⊘∾

A middle-aged man's waistline is his line of least resistance.

•⊙–⊘•

Middle age is that period when you are just as young as ever, but it takes a lot more effort.

MIDDLE OF THE ROAD

A fellow who tries to straddle an issue is like one in the middle of the highway, subject to being hit by both lines of traffic.

MIDGET

During the days of the Salem, Massachusetts, witch hunts, a midget was imprisoned for fortune-telling. She later escaped from jail, and the headline in the local newspaper read: SMALL MEDIUM AT LARGE.

MID-LIFE CRISIS

You'll have to excuse me but I'm going through a very difficult time in a man's life. I'm too tired to work and too broke to quit.

MILK

Milkman: Are you sure you want fifty-four quarts of milk?
Lady: Yes. My doctor told me to take a bath in milk.

Milkman: Do you want it pasteurized?
Lady: No, just up to my chin.

              ⊸—⊷

Scott: What makes this milk so blue?
Mike: It comes from discontented cows.

Millionaire

A billionaire after taxes.

Mind Your Own Business

To keep your teeth in good shape, mind your own business.

Minister

Mother: Quick, Henry, call the doctor. Johnny just swallowed a coin.
Father: I think we ought to send for the minister. He can get money out of anybody.

              ⊸—⊷

Wife: Who was that at the door, dear?
Husband: It was that new minister. He has been by four times this week.
Wife: What is his name?
Husband: I think it's Pester Smith.

              ⊸—⊷

Delivering a speech at a banquet on the night of his arrival in a large city, a visiting minister told several anecdotes he expected to repeat at meetings the next day. Because he wanted to use the jokes again, he requested that the reporters omit them from any accounts they might turn in to their newspapers. A cub reporter, in commenting on the speech, ended his piece with the following: "The minister told a number of stories that cannot be published."

◦❧—❧◦

Q: What is the difference between a doctor and a minister?
A: One practices and the other preaches.

◦❧—❧◦

While the minister was speaking a man fell asleep. The minister raised his voice and pounded the pulpit but the man would not wake up. Finally, the minister called to a deacon, "Go wake that man up."
The deacon replied, "Wake him up yourself. You put him to sleep!"

◦❧—❧◦

The minister of a large church asked the secretary to put his topic on the bulletin board so that everyone could see what his next Sunday's sermon would be. He said, "My topic is 'Are Ministers Cracking Up?'"
The secretary put up the following announcement: "Our Minister's Cracking Up."

◦❧—❧◦

Priest: Rabbi, when are you going to break down and eat ham?
Rabbi: At your wedding, Father.

◦❧—❧◦

The new minister stood at the church door greeting the members as they left the Sunday morning service. Most of the people were very generous in telling the new minister how they liked his message, except for one man who said, "That was a very dull and boring sermon, pastor."
In a few minutes the same man appeared again in the line and said, "I didn't think you did any preparation for your message, pastor."

Once again, the man appeared, this time muttering, "You really blew it. You didn't have a thing to say, pastor."

Finally the minister could stand it no longer. He went over to one of the deacons and inquired about the man.

"Oh, don't let that guy bother you," said the deacon. "He is a little slow. All he does is go around repeating whatever he hears other people saying."

∾⊸—⊶∾

After the funeral a minister posted this notice on the church bulletin board: "Brother Poure departed for heaven at 3:30 A.M."

The next day he found the following written below his announcement: "Heaven, 8:00 P.M.—Mr. Poure has not arrived yet. Great Anxiety."

∾⊸—⊶∾

Thirteen ministers were on a flight to New York. When they came into a large storm, they told the stewardess to tell the pilot that everything would be okay because thirteen ministers were on board.

Later the stewardess returned from the cockpit.

"What did the pilot say?" one preacher asked.

"He said he was glad to have thirteen ministers aboard but he would rather have four good engines."

∾⊸—⊶∾

Ministers fall into four categories:

1. Those who do not have any notes and the people have no idea how long they will speak.
2. Those who put down on the podium in front of them each page of their sermon as they read it. These honest ones enable the audience to keep track of how much more is to come.
3. Those who cheat by putting each sheet of notes under the others in their hand.
4. And, worst of all, those who put down each sheet of notes as they read it and then horrify the audience by picking up the whole batch and reading off the other side.

Mink

I promised my wife a mink for her birthday—if she'd keep his cage clean.

Minor Operation

One performed on somebody else.

Mirror

"I practice smiling in front of a mirror."
"I bet it works . . . I can't keep from laughing myself."

—◦—

"Is this one of your silly abstract paintings?"
"No, that's a mirror!"

—◦—

Mrs. Jones was standing in her kitchen with a friend. She looked out the window and pointed at the neighbor's wash hanging on the clothesline and said to her friend, "Just look at Mrs. Martin's wash. It sure looks dirty. Look at all those gray streaks on her laundry."

Her friend replied, "Those streaks aren't on your neighbor's wash—they're on your window!"

Misfit

In a small town everyone made fun of a local misfit. They would hold out a dime and a nickel to him and ask him which he wanted. He would always choose a nickel. One day somebody asked him why he always chose the nickel. The misfit replied, "If I ever took a dime, they'd quit giving me nickels."

Mistake

What a doctor buries.

◦−◦−◦

A well-adjusted person is one who makes the same mistake twice without getting nervous.

◦−◦−◦

Man: Pastor, do you think it is right for one man to profit from another man's mistake?
Pastor: Why, most certainly not!
Man: Then would you mind returning the twenty-five dollars I gave you last year for marrying me?

Model Husband

Always some other woman's.

Modesty

The art of encouraging others to find out for themselves how important you are.

Money

When someone says, "It's only money," it's usually your money he's talking about.

◦−◦−◦

Money used to talk—then it whispered. Now it just sneaks off.

◦−◦−◦

Most money is tainted. Taint yours and taint mine.

⚬

The easiest way to teach children the value of money is to borrow some from them.

⚬

Money has wings and most of us see only the tail feathers.

⚬

There's something bigger than money—bills.

⚬

Money brings only misery. But with money you can afford it.

⚬

Photographer (to young man): It will make a much better picture if you put your hand on your father's shoulder.
Father: It would be much more natural if he had his hand in my pocket.

⚬

Money isn't everything and don't let anybody tell you it is. There are other things such as stocks, bonds, letters of credit, traveler's checks, drafts . . .

⚬

Wife to husband: Of course I spend more than you make, dear. I have great confidence in you.

⚬

Money talks. It says good-bye.

⚬

Joe: Money doesn't bring happiness.
Moe: Can you prove it?
Joe: Sure, you take a guy with 40 million dollars. He ain't any happier than a man with 37 million dollars.

∽⊶—⊷∾

Credit manager: Are you going to pay us something on that account?
Customer: I can't just now.
Credit manager: If you don't, I'll tell all your other creditors that you paid us in full.

∽⊶—⊷∾

Blessed are the young, for they shall inherit the national debt.

∽⊶—⊷∾

It takes twice as much money to live beyond your means as it used to.

∽⊶—⊷∾

If the president asks me to tighten my belt again, I'm liable to end up with gangrene of the stomach.

∽⊶—⊷∾

Today a dollar saved is a quarter earned.

∽⊶—⊷∾

Two men both grabbed for the check after eating lunch together. The man to get the check said, "Either you're losing your grip, or I don't know my own strength."

∽⊶—⊷∾

Martin: Haven't you forgotten that you owe me five hundred dollars?

George: I should say not. Didn't you see me trying to duck into that alley to avoid you?

❦

Sign in store: "Cash only, please. We know that your check is good, but we don't trust the banks."

❦

Young man: I say, old man, could you lend me one dollar?
Old man: I'm a little deaf in that ear; go around to the other one.
Young man: Could you lend me five dollars?
Old man: Lend you what?
Young man: Five dollars.
Old man: Oh, you had better go back to the one-dollar ear.

❦

Show me a man who hides his wallet in the freezer, and I'll show you a guy who has cold cash to spend.

❦

Renter: I'll send you my check for the first of the month.
Manager: Could you give me a rough idea of what month?

❦

A theater manager found a wallet with no name and seven hundred dollars in it. He announced to the audience, "Will the person who lost the seven hundred dollars please form a double line at the box office?"

❦

The economy is terrible. At the beginning of the year, the politicians promised things would improve by the last quarter. Well, I'm down to my last quarter and they haven't improved.

❦

Reporter: Mr. Paul Getty, you are a very wealthy man. Would you say that your holdings would be worth a billion dollars?

Mr. Getty: I suppose so, but remember: A billion doesn't go as far as it used to.

⚬—⚬

Visitor: Where is the capital of the USA?
Native: Spread all over the world.

⚬—⚬

I hope they don't raise the standard of living any higher. I can't afford it now.

MONOLOGUE

Son: What is a monologue, Dad?
Dad: That's a conversation between a husband and a wife.
Son: But our teacher said that was a dialogue.
Dad: Your teacher isn't married.

MOODS

My husband has three moods . . . hungry, thirsty, and both.

MORNING

I hate mornings . . . they're so early.

⚬—⚬

If the Lord wanted us to enjoy sunrises, they would come at ten o'clock in the morning.

MORTGAGE

A small house is better than a large mortgage.

MOTHER-IN-LAW

My mother-in-law sent me two sweaters for Christmas. When she came for a visit, I put on one of the sweaters. The first thing she said was, "What's the matter? Didn't you like the other one?"

☙——❧

I didn't mind it when my wife and my mother-in-law both said, "I do" at the wedding . . . but when I had to carry the two of them over the threshold, that was too much.

☙——❧

A woman who is never outspoken.

MOTHERS AND FATHERS

Mother to fussy son: Twenty years from now you'll be telling some girl what a great cook your mother was . . . now eat your dinner.

☙——❧

Parents spend the first part of a child's life urging him to walk and talk, and the rest of his childhood making him sit down and keep quiet.

☙——❧

The quickest way for a parent to get a child's attention is to sit down and look comfortable.

☙——❧

A mother of twelve was asked how in the world she could take care of all her children.

"Well," she replied. "When I only had one it took all my time, so how could eleven more make any difference?"

◦◦—◦◦

Little boy (calling father at office): Hello, who is this?
Father (recognizing son's voice): The smartest man in the world.
Little boy: Pardon me; I got the wrong number.

◦◦—◦◦

A six-year-old ran up and down the supermarket aisles shouting frantically, "Marian, Marian."

Finally reunited with his mother, he was chided by her, "You shouldn't call me 'Marian.' I'm your mother, you know."

"I know," he replied, "but the store is full of mothers."

MOTHER'S DAY

Mother's Day brings back memories of maternal advice and admonition. Picture the scene with these famous offspring.

Alexander the Great's mother: How many times do I have to tell you—you can't have everything you want in this world!

Franz Schubert's mother: Take my advice, son. Never start anything you can't finish.

Achilles' mother: Stop imagining things. There's nothing wrong with your heel.

Madame de Pompadour's mother: For heaven's sake, child, do something about your hair!

Sigmund Freud's mother: Stop pestering me! I've told you a hundred times the stork brought you!

MOTIVATION

A young man had a job with a company that required him to work very late at night. In going home after work, he found that it was fastest to walk through a cemetery near his home. One night when he was very tired, he accidentally fell into a freshly dug grave.

At first he was not too concerned, but when he realized that he could not get out because the hole was too deep, he became somewhat hysterical. Finally, in complete exhaustion, he sat down in the corner of the grave and fell asleep.

Shortly thereafter another man decided to walk through the cemetery and happened to fall into the same grave. He too went through great effort to get out but could not. He then moved around the grave until he stepped on the first man who was asleep. The first man woke up and shouted, "You can't get out of here."

But he did.

Mouse

Teacher: Robert Burns wrote "To a Field Mouse."
Student: I'll bet he didn't get an answer.

Movie

Wife: I thought the movie and the acting stank!
Husband: I can't say I liked it that well.

❧ ❧

Actor: Do come and see my picture and you'll leave the theater a happier man.
Friend: Yes, I always do feel much better after a good sleep.

❧ ❧

I went to one of those new movies last week. It was so bloody that it was rated "O-positive."

Music

He was escorting his wife to a concert and they arrived late. "What are they playing," he whispered to his neighbor.
"The Fifth Symphony," replied the man.

"Well, thank goodness," sighed the husband. "I've missed four of them anyway."

◦—◦

A married couple trying to live up to a snobbish life-style went to a party. The conversation turned to Mozart. "Absolutely brilliant, magnificent, a genius!"

The woman, wanting to join in the conversation, remarked casually, "Ah, Mozart. You're so right. I love him. Only this morning I saw him getting on the No. 5 bus going to Coney Island." There was a sudden hush, and everyone looked at her. Her husband was mortified. He pulled her away and whispered, "We're leaving right now. Get your coat and let's get out of here."

As they drove home, he kept muttering to himself. Finally his wife turned to him. "You're angry about something."

"Oh really? You noticed?" he sneered. "I've never been so embarrassed in my life! You saw Mozart take the No. 5 bus to Coney Island? You idiot! Don't you know the No. 5 bus doesn't go to Coney Island?"

◦—◦

Nowadays, whatever is not worth saying is sung.

◦—◦

"Are you fond of music?"
"Yes, but keep right on playing."

◦—◦

Notice in the church bulletin: "Mrs. Smith will sink two numbers. She will be accompanied by the choir."

Muzzled

A bear never knows until he is muzzled how many people are not afraid of him.

MY WIFE

I wouldn't say my wife is a poor housekeeper, but she doesn't turn on the stove. She just lights the grease.

—⊙—

Customer: I've come back to buy that television I was looking at yesterday.
Salesman: That's good. May I ask what the one dominating thing was that made you want this set?
Customer: My wife.

—⊙—

I don't know what to get my wife anymore. First she wanted a mink; I got her a mink. Then she wanted a silver fox; I got her a silver fox. It was ridiculous . . . the house was full of animals.

—⊙—

My wife just had plastic surgery . . . I took away all her credit cards.

—⊙—

My wife talks so much I get hoarse just listening to her.

—⊙—

My wife is the sweetest, most tolerant, most beautiful woman in the world. This is a paid political announcement.

—⊙—

I walked into a store and said, "This is my wife's birthday. I'd like to buy her a beautiful fountain pen."
The clerk winked at me and said, "A little surprise, eh?"
I said, "Yes, she's expecting a Cadillac."

—⊙—

"My wife always has the last word."
"You're lucky. Mine never gets to it."

❦

"One day my wife drove up the side of a building and there was another woman driver coming down."

❦

"Every once in awhile my wife puts on one of those mud packs."
"Does it improve her looks?"
"Only for a few days—then the mud falls off!"

❦

"Why are you adding up those figures?"
"My wife said she is going to lose four pounds a month. I figure that in thirty-two months I'll be rid of her!"

❦

My wife thinks she's Teddy Roosevelt. She runs from store to store, yelling, "*Charge!*"

❦

"My wife has been cooking a chicken for two days."
"For two days?"
"Yeah! The cookbook said to cook it one-half-hour to the pound—and my wife weighs 110 pounds!"

❦

Bob: My wife treats me like an idol.
Ray: Why do you say that?
Bob: She feeds me burnt offerings at meals.

❦

"My wife says if I don't chuck golf, she'll leave me!"
"That's too bad."
"Yes, I'll miss her."

∽❍—❍∾

I miss my wife's cooking . . . as often as I can.

∽❍—❍∾

My wife's meals are something to behold . . . not to eat, just behold.

MYSTIC

Attendant: Do you wish to consult with Wing Tong Fong, the great Chinese mystic?

Lady: Yes, tell him his mother is here from the Bronx.

❧ N ❧

Nag

A woman with no horse sense.

❧❧

Man: Do you serve breakfast here?
Waitress: Sure; what'll it be?
Man: Let me have watery scrambled eggs . . . and some burnt toast . . . and some weak coffee, lukewarm.
Waitress: Whatever you say, sir.
Man: Now, are you doing anything while that order is going through?
Waitress: Why—no, sir.
Man: Then sit here and nag me awhile . . . I'm homesick!

Nails

"Do you file your nails?"
"No, I just cut them off and throw them away."

Name

First cowboy: My name's Tex.
Second cowboy: You from Texas?
First cowboy: Nope, I'm from Louisiana, but who wants to be called Louise?

❧❧

If you are looking for a name for a new pet, try one of these:

A white mouse	Mousey Tung
A collie	Flower

A collie	Melon
A boxer	Shorts
A rabbit	Transit
A donkey	Shane
A pigeon	Toad
A frog	Horn
A horse	Greeley
A rooster	Shire Sos
A gopher	Broke
A crow	Magnon
A kitten	Kaboodle
A cat	Mandu
A rat	Frank Lloyd
A rat	Fink

∽⊙—⊙∿

Lady of the house: I want you to stand at the front door and call the guests' names as they arrive.

Butler: Very well, madam. I've been wanting to do that for years.

Natural Selection

To take the largest piece.

Nearsighted

Jack: I'm so nearsighted I nearly worked myself to death.

Elmer: What's being nearsighted got to do with working yourself to death?

Jack: I couldn't tell whether the boss was watching me or not, so I had to work all the time.

Neighbor

The man in the repair shop said, "Here it is, Mr. Wilson. Your lawnmower is now in perfect condition. Just one precaution, however.

Don't ever lend it to a neighbor."

"That's just the trouble," said Mr. Wilson. "I am the neighbor."

∽◦—◦∾

Mother: I don't think the man upstairs likes Mike to play on his drums.

Father: Why do you say that?

Mother: Because this afternoon he gave Mike a knife and asked him if he knew what was inside the drum.

∽◦—◦∾

The only people who listen to both sides of an argument are the neighbors.

Nervous

He's so nervous, he keeps coffee awake.

∽◦—◦∾

I got nervous after the copilot asked me how to get to the cockpit.

∽◦ ◦∾

"Excuse me for being nervous," the sheriff apologized as he slipped the noose over the condemned man's head. "This is my first hanging.

Man: "Mine too!"

News

Wife to husband: Shall we watch the six o'clock news and get indigestion, or wait for the eleven o'clock news and have insomnia?

∽◦—◦∾

A rich newspaper owner decided to give his newspaper to one of his three sons. He told them that he would give the paper to the one who could come up with the most sensational headline of only three words. The following is what they came up with:

First son: REAGAN TURNS COMMUNIST!

Second son: KHOMEINI BECOMES CHRISTIAN!

The winner was the third son who submitted only two words:

Third son: POPE ELOPES.

A newspaper once carried an editorial which stated bluntly that half the city council were crooks. Under threat of arrest, the editor issued the following retraction: "Half the city council aren't crooks."

NICKEL

If a nickel knew what it is worth today, it would feel like two cents.

About all you can get with a nickel these days is heads or tails.

NIGHT SCHOOL

Did you hear about the graduation ceremony at night school? Everybody wore a nightcap and nightgown.

NITRATE

Cheapest price for calling long-distance.

NO BOTHER

"Don't bother showing me to the door."

"It's no bother . . . it's a pleasure!"

Noah

Noah's remark as the animals were boarding the ark: Now I've heard everything.

<hr />

Teacher: Do you know who built the ark?
Student: No.
Teacher: Correct.

<hr />

Noah was standing at the gangplank checking off the pairs of animals when he saw three camels trying to get on board.

"Wait a minute!" said Noah. "Two each is the limit. One of you will have to stay behind."

"It won't be me," said the first camel. "I'm the camel whose back is broken by the last straw."

"I'm the one people swallow while straining at a gnat," said the second.

"I," said the third, "am the one that shall pass through the eye of a needle sooner than a rich man shall enter heaven."

"Come on in," said Noah, "the world is going to need all of you."

Nonsense

A little nonsense now and then,
Is relished by the wisest men.

Noodle Soup

Customer: Yes, I know that fish is brain food. But I don't care much for fish. Isn't there some other kind of brain food?
Waiter: Well, there's noodle soup.

NOTE

The following note was fastened to a defective parking meter by a rubber band:

"I put three nickels in this meter. License number 4761PQ."

"FRD719. Me, too!"

"So did I. JRY335."

"I'm not going to pay a nickel to find out if these guys are lying. WTM259."

NOTHING

Most of us know how to say nothing . . . few of us know when.

NUDITY

Phyllis Diller says there's so much nudity in films that this year's Oscar for clothing design will probably go to a dermatologist.

NUTS

There are more men than women in mental institutions—which goes to show who's driving whom nuts.

❦

A pastor got this note accompanying a box of goodies, addressed to him and his wife, from an elderly lady in the church.

Dear Pastor,

Knowing that you do not eat sweets, I am sending the candy to your wife—and nuts to you.

O

OARS

The fellow who's busy pulling on the oars hasn't got time to rock the boat.

OBEDIENCE

He that has learned to obey will know how to command.

⁕

There are two kinds of men who never amount to much: those who cannot do what they are told, and those who can do nothing else.

⁕

One of the first things one notices in a backward country is that children are still obeying their parents.

OBSCENE

What is this world coming to? I hear they just arrested a fellow who talks dirty to plants. Caught him making an obscene fern call!

OBSTETRICIAN

Sign in an obstetrician's office: "Pay-as-you-grow."

ODD

First boy: My dad is an Odd Fellow.
Second boy: Your mother is quite a peculiar character also.

Offering

An usher was passing the collection plate at a large church wedding. One of those attending looked up, very puzzled. Without waiting for the question, the usher nodded his head, "I know it's unusual, but the father of the bride requested it."

∽ତ—ତৎ

Mother: Now remember to put some of your allowance in the offering at church.

Son: Why not buy an ice cream cone with it and let the cashier put it in the offering?

∽ତ—ତৎ

Minister before the morning offering: The Lord owns the cattle on a thousand hills. He only needs cowboys to round them up. Will the ushers please come forward for the offering?

Office Sign

In a very busy office there were three boxes for mail marked *Urgent*, *Frantic*, and *Most Frantic*.

Ohio

Teacher: Who discovered America?

Student: Ohio.

Teacher: Ohio? That's ridiculous. It was Columbus.

Student: Yes, sir. I know. But I didn't think it was necessary to mention the gentleman's first name, sir.

Old

You're getting old if the gleam in your eye is the sun hitting your bifocals.

∽ତ—ତৎ

My husband is so old that he remembers Eve when she was just a rib.

❦

Growing old doesn't seem so bad when you consider the alternative.

❦

A trim-looking octogenarian was asked how he maintained his slim figure. "I get my exercise acting as a pallbearer for all my friends who exercise."

❦

"My grandfather is ninety-five years old and every day he goes horseback riding—except during the month of July."
"Why not during July?"
"Because that is when the man who puts him on the horse goes on his vacation."

❦

As you grow older you make a fool of yourself in a more dignified manner.

❦

You can tell you are getting older when:
You sit in a rocking chair and can't get it going.
You burn the midnight oil after 8:00 P.M.
You look forward to a dull evening.
Your knees buckle and your belt won't.
Your little black book contains only names ending in M.D.
Your back goes out more than you do.
You decide to procrastinate and never get around to it.
Dialing long-distance wears you out.
You walk with your head held high, trying to get used to your bifocals.
You sink your teeth into a steak and they stay there.

❦

"Why do you keep reading your Bible all day long?" a youngster demanded of his aged grandfather.

"Well," he explained, "you might say I was cramming for my final examinations."

❦

Whenever a man's friends begin to compliment him about looking young, he may be sure that they think he is growing old.
—*Washington Irving*

❦

Patient: How can I live to be a hundred, doctor?
Doctor: Give up cookies, cake, and ice cream. Stop eating red meat, potatoes, and bread. And no soft drinks.
Patient: And if I do that, I will live to be a hundred?
Doctor: Maybe not, but it will certainly seem like it.

❦

More people would live to a ripe old age if they weren't too busy providing for it.

❦

Young man: Why did you live to be the age of 115?
Old man: Mainly because I was born in 1876.

Old Car

Willy: Why did you bury your old car?
Billy: Well, the battery was dead, the pistons were shot, and then the engine died.

Old Faithful

He: Where are you going on your vacation?
Him: Yellowstone National Park.

He: Don't forget Old Faithful.
Him: She's going with me.

Old Nature

A man was taken to court for stealing an item from a store. The man said to the judge, "Your Honor, I'm a Christian. I've become a new man. But I have an old nature also. It was not my new man who did wrong. It was my old man."

The judge responded, "Since it was the old man that broke the law, we'll sentence him to sixty days in jail. And since the new man was an accomplice in the theft, we'll give him thirty days also. I therefore sentence you both to ninety days in jail."

One Foot

Some speakers and most listeners would approve of the rule among certain tribes in Africa. Their regulation is that when a man rises to speak he must stand on one foot while delivering his speech. The minute the lifted foot touches the ground, the speech ends—or the speaker is forcibly silenced.

One-Half

Trying hard to get on a bus, a woman snapped at the man in back of her, "If you were half a man, you'd help me onto this bus." He answered, "If you were half a lady, you wouldn't need any help."

One-Track

Most people operate on a one-track mind of two rails—"*me*" and "*I*."

Oops

Man: Just look at that young person with the short hair and blue jeans. Is it a boy or a girl?

Bystander: It's a girl; she's my daughter.
Man: Oh, please forgive me, sir. I had no idea you were her father.
Bystander: I'm not. I'm her mother.

⸰⊷——⊶⸰

A tired guest at a formal function spoke to the man next to him: "Gee, this thing is a bore; I'm going to beat it!"
"I would, too," said the man, "but I've got to stay. I'm the host!"

OPERATION

Joe: I'm afraid I can't afford that operation now.
Moe: It looks like you'll have to talk about your old one for another year.

⸰⊷——⊶⸰

When I got the bill for my operation, I found out why they wear masks in the operating room.

⸰⊷——⊶⸰

Surgeons invited to dinner parties are often asked to carve the meat—or worse yet, to watch the host carve while commenting on the surgeon's occupation. At one party, a surgeon friend was watching the carving while his host kept up a running commentary—"How am I doing, doc? How do you like that technique? I'd make a pretty good surgeon, don't you think?"

When the host finished and the slices of meat lay neatly on the serving platter, the surgeon spoke up: "Anybody can take them apart, Harry. Now let's see you put them back together again."

OPERETTA

Q: What is an operetta?
A: A girl who works for the telephone company.

Opportunity

When your automobile engine develops a knock, chances are it's opportunity knocking for some mechanic.

∽⊖—⊖∾

"May I ask you the secret of your success?"
"There is no easy street. You just jump at your opportunity."
"But how can I tell when my opportunity comes?"
"You can't. You've got to keep on jumping."

∽⊖—⊖∾

The trouble with opportunity is that it's always more recognizable going than coming.

Opposites

Your problem: When you get angry, it is because you are ill-tempered.
My situation: It just happens that my nerves are bothering me.

∽⊖—⊖∾

Your problem: When you don't like someone, it is because you are prejudiced.
My situation: I happen to be a good judge of human nature.

∽⊖—⊖∾

Your problem: When you compliment someone, it is because you use flattery.
My situation: I only encourage folks.

Optimist

A person who thinks humorists will eventually run out of definitions of an optimist.

∽⊖—⊖∾

He who thinks a housefly is looking for the way out.

∾⊙—⊙∾

A man who goes into a restaurant without a dime and figures on paying for the meal with the pearl he hopes to find in the oyster.

∾⊙—⊙∾

Twixt optimist and pessimist
The difference is droll;
The optimist sees the doughnut,
The pessimist the hole.

ORANGES

Customer: Three of those oranges you sent me were rotten. I'll bring them back.
Merchant: That's all right, you needn't bring them back. Your word is just as good as the oranges.

ORATOR

One who misses many fine opportunities for keeping quiet.

ORDEAL

What some ideal marriages turn out to be.

ORGANIST

The organist wanted to make an impression on the visiting clergy-man with her musical accomplishment. She wrote a note to the old sex-ton who had been a little slack in his work of pumping enough air for the organ, and handed it to him just before the service started. But, making a natural mistake, the sexton passed the note on to the visiting clergyman, who opened it and read: "Keep blowing away until I give the signal to stop."

ORTHOPEDIST

Orthopedists get all the breaks.

OUT OF BUSINESS

Going out of business has become so profitable for one merchant that he's opening a chain of going-out-of-business stores.

OVERCOAT

A meek little man in a restaurant timidly touched the arm of a man putting on an overcoat. "Excuse me," he said, "but do you happen to be Mr. Smith of Newport?"

"No, I'm not!" the man answered impatiently.

"Oh-er-well," stammered the first man, "you see, I am, and that's his overcoat you're putting on."

OVEREATING

The destiny that shapes our ends.

OVERTIME

Employer: How long did you work at your other job?

Job seeker: Fifty-five years.

Employer: How old are you?

Job seeker: Forty-five.

Employer: How could you work fifty-five years when you are only forty-five years old?

Job seeker: Overtime.

✣ P ✣

Pain in the Neck

"How is the pain in your neck?"
"He's out playing golf."

❦—❧

The man who thinks he knows it all is a pain in the neck to those of us who really do.

Painting

Phil: Aren't you rather warm doing your painting all bundled up like that?
Bill: Well, it says right here on the paint can to be sure to put on three coats.

Panama Canal

An inside strait.

Pants

Pants are made for men and not for women. Women are made for men and not for pants. When a man pants for a woman and a woman pants for a man, that makes a pair of pants. Pants are like molasses: they are thinner in hot weather and thicker in cold weather. There has been much discussion as to whether pants is singular or plural; but it seems to us that when men wear pants it's plural, and when they don't, it's singular. If you want to make the pants last, make the coat first.

❦—❧

Kenny: I just bought a new suit with two pairs of pants.
Lenny: Well, how do you like it?
Kenny: Fine, only it's too hot wearing two pairs.

PARADISE

Two ivory cubes with dots all over them.

PARENTS

Wrinkles are hereditary. Parents get them from their children.

∽⚬—⚬∾

I've wanted to run away from home more often since I've had kids than when I was a boy.

∽⚬—⚬∾

My parents are in the iron and steel business. Mom irons and Dad steals.

PARKING SPACE

Unoccupied space on the other side of the street.

PARSON

The parson of a tiny congregation in Arkansas disappeared one night with the entire church treasury, and the local constable set out to capture him. This he did, dragging the culprit back by the collar a week later. "Here's the varmint, folks," announced the constable grimly. "I'm sorry to say he's already squandered our money, but I drug him back so we can make him preach it out."

∽⚬—⚬∾

Operator: Do you wish to make a station-to-station call, sir?
Minister: No, parson-to-parson.

PASSION

Passion makes idiots of the cleverest men, and makes the biggest idiots clever.

PASSPORT PHOTO

A way to see yourself as others see you.

PASTOR

Friend: Pastor, how do you let off steam when you miss a shot and your golf ball goes into a sand trap?
Pastor: I just repeat the names of some of the members of my congregation . . . with feeling!

❦

Friend: Say, pastor, how is it that you're so thin and gaunt while your horse is so fat and sleek?
Pastor: Because I feed the horse and the congregation feeds me.

❦

Did you hear about the young pastor who fouled up the established routine? He didn't stand at the door and shake hands with the worshipers after the service. He went out to the curb and shook hands with the red-faced parents waiting for their children to come out of Sunday school.

❦

The pastor asked his congregation to participate in the morning offering and said, "Let us give generously—according to what you reported on your income tax."

❦

When the assistant pastor made the announcements he said, "The pastor will be gone tonight, and we will be having a service of singing and praise."

∾⊙—⊙∾

Notice in the church bulletin: There will be no healing service this Sunday due to the pastor's illness.

∾⊙—⊙∾

Remark to the pastor after the morning service: Every sermon you preach is better than the next one.

∾⊙—⊙∾

Greg: We call our pastor Reverend. What do you call yours?
Fred: We call ours Neverend.

∾⊙—⊙∾

Our pastor suffers from foot-and-mouth disease: He won't visit and he can't preach.

∾⊙—⊙∾

A pastor, burdened by the importance of his work, went into the sanctuary to pray. Falling to his knees, he lamented, "O Lord, I am nothing! I am nothing!"

The minister of education passed by, and overhearing the prayer, was moved to join the pastor on his knees. Shortly he, too, was crying aloud, "O Lord, I too am nothing. I am nothing."

The janitor of the church, awed by the sight of the two men praying, joined them, crying, "O Lord, I also am nothing. I am nothing."

At this, the minister of education nudged the pastor and said, "Now look who thinks he's nothing!"

∾⊙—⊙∾

Frances: What do you think of our new pastor?

Sharon: On six days of the week he is invisible, and on the seventh day he is incomprehensible.

∞—∞

The minister's little daughter was sent to bed with a stomachache and missed her usual romp with her daddy. A few minutes later she appeared at the top of the stairs and called to her mother, "Mama, let me talk with Daddy."

"No, my dear, not tonight. Get back in bed."

"Please Mama."

"I said no. That's enough now."

"Mother, I'm a very sick woman, and I must see my pastor at once."

∞—∞

An elderly woman was weeping as she bade good-bye to the man who had been pastor of her church for several years.

"My dear lady," consoled the departing pastor, "don't get so upset. The bishop surely will send a much better pastor to replace me here."

"That's what they told us the last time," wailed the woman.

PATIENCE

It is easy finding reasons why other folks should be patient.

∞—∞

Patience is the art of concealing your impatience.

∞—∞

Patience is the ability to "count down" before "blasting off."

PAWNBROKER

One who lives off the flat of the land.

PAYMENTS

Rod: I've got the worst kind of car trouble anybody could have.
Ron: What kind is it?
Rod: The engine won't start and the payments won't stop.

〜◦—◦〜

The latest thing for a man who has everything is a calendar to remind him when the payments are due.

PEASHOOTER

A baby blowgun.

PEDESTRIAN

A father who has kids who can drive.

PEEKABOO

The act of spying on a ghost.

PEN

There's no wound deeper than a pen can give;
It makes men living dead, and dead men live.

PENNY A POINT

A man arrived home early to find his wife in the arms of his best friend. The best friend commented how much he and the man's wife were in love with each other.

"Tell you what I'll do," said the best friend. "I'll play a game of cards for her. If I win, you divorce her, and if you win, I promise never to see her again. O.K.? How about playing gin rummy?"

"That's all right with me," agreed the husband. "And how about a penny a point to make the game a bit interesting?"

Perfect Pair

Husband: Nancy and Mike make a perfect pair, don't you think?
Wife: Yes. He's a pill and she's a headache.

Perfection

The closest anyone comes to perfection is when he or she fills out a job application form.

Period Furniture

"Give an example of period furniture."
"Well, I should say an electric chair because it ends a sentence."

Pessimist

No one ought to be so pessimistic he can't see some good in the other fellow's troubles.

∞⊝—⊝∞

A pessimist is a person who grows his own crabgrass.

∞⊝—⊝∞

A lot of pessimists get that way from financing optimists.

∞⊝—⊝∞

A pessimist on world conditions had insomnia so bad the sheep were picketing him for shorter hours.

∞⊝—⊝∞

A pessimist complains about the noise made when opportunity knocks.

PET ROCK

Larry: My father won't let me have a pet rock.
Steve: Why not?
Larry: He's afraid it might have pebbles.

PHILOSOPHY

Unintelligible answers to insoluble problems.

PHONY

First husband: I bought my wife a string of pearls for her birthday.
Second husband: Why didn't you buy her something practical like a car?
First husband: Did you ever hear of a phony car?

PHOTOGRAPH ALBUMS

The strange views people take of things.

PIANO

Jack: My wife used to play the piano a lot, but since the children came she doesn't have time.
Mack: Children are a comfort, aren't they?

∽―∾

Mark: My brother has been playing the piano for three years.
Clark: Aren't his fingers tired?

PICKPOCKET

Someone who never learned to keep his hands to himself.

⚬─⚬─⚬

Jack: Somebody picked my pocket.
Mack: What did he get?
Jack: Practice.

⚬─⚬─⚬

Pete: Does your wife pick your suits?
Mike: No, just my pockets.

PIERCED EARS

"Have you ever had your ears pierced?"
"No, but I have often had them bored."

PIG TOES

In a small town the farmers of the community had gotten together to discuss some important issues. About midway through the meeting a wife of one of the farmers stood up and spoke her peace.

One old farmer stood up and said, "What does she know about anything. I would like to ask her if she knows how many toes a pig has?"

Quick as a flash the woman replied, "Take off your boots, man, and count them!"

PIGS

A city family decided to spend their vacation on a farm for the experience. The only thing they did not like was the noise that the pigs made.

The father wrote to the farmer the next year about coming again for another vacation. He asked if the pigs were still there. He received the following note from the farmer.

"Don't worry. We haven't had pigs on the farm since you were here."

∽⊙—⊙∾

"Do you know anything about pigs?"
"My father raised a big hog once."
"You're telling me."

PILLS

A patient limped into the doctor's office. The doctor handed the patient a large pill. Just then his nurse asked him some questions. The patient limped over to the sink and choked down the pill. Then the doctor returned with a bucket and said, "Now drop the pill in the bucket and we'll soak your foot."

PIN

Lem: I just sat down on a pin.
Clem: Did it hurt?
Lem: No, it was a safety pin.

PINE TREE

A tree that mopes.

PITCHFORK

In defending a client charged with assault, a lawyer told the jury his client was walking down the road with a pitchfork on his shoulder. A large dog that was very fierce attacked the man, and the man killed the dog with the pitchfork.

"Why did you kill my dog?" demanded the dog's owner.
"Because he tried to bite me."
"But why did you not go at him with the other end of the pitchfork?"
"Why didn't your dog come at me with his other end?"

PLAGIARISM

When you take stuff from one writer, it's plagiarism; but when you take it from many writers, it's research.
—*Wilson Mizner*

PLANE

Customer: Where is your plane?
Pilot: Over there—the tri-motor plane.
Customer: What do you mean tri-motor plane?
Pilot: If one motor goes bad, we'll try the other.

PLANTS

In the potted-plant section of a Fresno, California, nursery: "Please don't talk to the plants unless you're going to buy."

❧ ❦ ❧

Wife: Plants grow faster if you talk to them.
Husband: But I don't know how to speak Geranium.

PLEASURE

"Don't bother showing me to the door."
"It's no bother—it's a pleasure!"

❧ ❦ ❧

First employee: Are you going to the boss's funeral?
Second employee: Oh, no, I'm working today. My motto is business before pleasure.

PLEDGE

The deacon ran into the pastor's office and exclaimed excitedly, "Pastor, I have terrible news to report! Burglars must've broken in last night. They stole $90,000 worth of pledges!"

PLUMBER

Walter: Who put that statue under the sink?
Frances: That's no statue. That's the plumber.

⁓o—e⁓

Is it true that plumbers' fantasies are called pipe dreams?

⁓o—e⁓

Householder: Well, I see you brought your tools with you.
Plumber: Yeah, I'm getting more absentminded every day.

POET

A poet has a great imagination—he imagines people will read his poems.

POISON

A young mother paying a visit to a doctor friend and his wife made no attempt to restrain her five-year-old son, who was ransacking an adjoining room. But, finally, an extra loud clatter of bottles did prompt her to say, "I hope, doctor, you don't mind Johnny being in there."

"No," said the doctor calmly. "He'll be quiet when he gets to the poisons."

POLICE

A candidate for the police force was being verbally examined. "If you were by yourself in a police car and were pursued by a desperate gang of criminals in another car doing forty miles an hour along a lonely road, what would you do?"

The candidate looked puzzled for a moment. Then he replied, "Fifty."

⁓o—e⁓

A jeweler watched as a huge truck pulled out in front of his store. The back came down and an elephant walked out. It broke one of the windows with its tusk and then using the trunk like a vacuum cleaner sucked up all the jewelry. The elephant then got back into the truck and it disappeared out of sight. When the jeweler finally regained his senses he called the police. The detectives came, and he told them his story.

"Could you describe the elephant?"

"An elephant is an elephant. You see one you've seen them all. What do you mean, 'describe him?'" asked the jeweler.

"Well," said the policeman, "there are two kinds of elephants, African and Indian. The Indian elephant has smaller ears and is not as large as the African elephant."

The jeweler said, "I can't help you out; he had a stocking pulled over his head."

※———※

Officer: Miss, you were doing over sixty miles an hour!

Sweet young thing: Oh, isn't that neat. I only learned to drive yesterday.

※———※

Things are so bad in our town that the police department now has an unlisted telephone number.

※———※

Show me a policewoman with children and I will show you a pistol-packing mama.

※———※

"Could you get that crook to confess to the crime?" asked the police chief.

"We tried everything, sir. We browbeat and badgered him with every question we could think of."

POLITE

A polite man is one who listens with interest to things he knows all about when they are told to him by a person who knows nothing about them.

POLITICS

After a political rally, a wife came home late and sank into a chair. "Everything is going great. We are going to sweep the country."

To which her husband responded, "Why not start with the living room?"

❦

A politician was giving a speech in a rural district when a yokel tossed a cabbage onto the platform. The quick-thinking politician gave it a sidelong glance and said, "It appears that one of my opponents has lost his head."

❦

Politicians are the same all over. They promise to build a bridge even when there is no river.

—*Nikita Khrushchev*

❦

We need a law that will permit a voter to sue a candidate for breach of promise.

❦

Political orator: Yes, I have heard the voice of the people calling me to duty.

Heckler: Maybe it was an echo.

❦

"Well, election time will soon be here. I plan to run for office again. I guess the air will soon be full of my speeches."

"Yeah! . . . and vice versa!"

***

The most promising of all careers.

***

All political parties die at last of swallowing their own lies.

***

The difference between a Republican and a Democrat: One is IN and the other is OUT.

***

Some go into politics not to do good, but to do well.

***

There's one thing the Democrats and Republicans share in common— our money.

—*Woody Allen*

Polygamy

A Mormon acquaintance once pushed Mark Twain into an argument on the issue of polygamy. After long and tedious expositions justifying the practice, the Mormon demanded that Twain cite any passage of Scripture expressly forbidding polygamy.

"Nothing easier," Twain replied. "'No man can serve two masters.'"

Poor Box

The minister's brain is often the "poor box" of the church.

Poor Preacher

Preacher: Please take it easy on the bill for repairing my car. Remember, I am a poor preacher.
Mechanic: I know; I heard you Sunday!

Popover

The thing that happens when you put too much corn in the corn popper.

Possessions

The wise man carries his possessions within him.

Postcard

The following postcard was received:

Dear George,
We both miss you as much as if you were right here.

Postponed

When I was a boy, I'd rather be licked twice than postponed once.

Pot Roast

I've heard so much about the bad effects of marijuana I'm afraid to eat pot roast.

Potato

Did you hear about the man who crossed a potato with a sponge? It wasn't especially good eating, but it sure held a lot of gravy.

∽⊙─⊙

Q: Why did the potatoes argue all the time?
A: They couldn't see eye-to-eye about anything.

POVERTY

State of mind sometimes induced by a neighbor's new car.

❧—☙

"Dad, what protects a man best from running wild . . . advice, restrictive law, or stern counsel?"
"Poverty, son, poverty."

PRACTICAL

City slicker: Is it right to say "a hen lays" or "a hen lies" eggs?
Farmer: Where I come from, the people just lift her up to see.

PRACTICE

Daughter: Mom, may I have some money for a new dress?
Mother: Ask your father, dear. You are getting married in a month and the practice would do you good.

PRAISE THE LORD

Did you hear about the country parson who decided to buy himself a horse? The dealer assured him that the one he selected was a perfect choice. "This here horse," he said, "has lived all his life in a religious atmosphere. So remember that he'll never start if you order 'Giddyap.' You've got to say, 'Praise the Lord.' Likewise, a 'Whoa' will never make him stop. You've got to say, 'Amen.'

Thus forewarned, the parson paid for the horse, mounted him, and with a cheery "Praise the Lord" sent him cantering off in the direction of the parson's parish. Suddenly, however, he noticed that the road ahead had been washed out, leaving a chasm two hundred yards deep. In a panic, he forgot his instructions and cried "Whoa" in vain several times.

The horse just cantered on. At the very last moment he remembered to cry "Amen" . . . and the horse stopped short at the very brink of the chasm. But alas! That's when the parson, out of force of habit, murmured fervently, "Praise the Lord!"

PRAYER

An ocean liner was sinking and the captain yelled, "Does anybody know how to pray?"

A minister on board said, "I do."

"Good," said the captain. "You start praying. The rest of us will put on the life belts. We are one belt short."

&ox—&co;

One friend to another: "You drive the car and I'll pray."

"What's the matter; don't you trust my driving?"

"Don't you trust my praying?"

&ox—&co;

Little Dennis began falling out of a tree and cried, "Lord, save me, save me!" There was a pause and he said, "Never mind, Lord, my pants just caught on a branch."

&ox—&co;

A little girl told her mother that her brother had set traps to catch poor, harmless birds. The mother asked if she had done anything about it.

"Oh, yes," the girl replied, "I prayed that the traps might not catch the birds."

"Anything else?"

"Yes, then I prayed that God would keep the birds from getting into the traps."

"Was that all?"

"Then I went and kicked the traps all to pieces."

&ox—&co;

A farmer was in town at noon and went into a restaurant for a hamburger and french fries. When he was served, he quietly bowed his head and gave the Lord thanks for his food.

Some rough-looking fellows at the next table saw him and thought they would give him a hard time. One of them called out, "Hey, farmer, does everyone do that where you live?"

"No, son," answered the farmer, "the pigs and donkeys don't."

⌘

Daughter: Why is everyone getting down on their knees in church?
Mother: Shhh, they are going to say their prayers.
Daughter: With all their clothes on?

⌘

Noticing that just before the football game started both teams gathered together and prayed briefly, a fan, seated next to a minister, asked what he thought would happen if both teams prayed with equal faith and fervor.

"In that event," replied the minister, "I imagine the Lord would simply sit back and enjoy one fine game of football."

⌘

Little Susie concluded her prayer by saying, "Dear God, before I finish, please take care of Daddy, take care of Mommy, take care of my baby brother, Grandma and Grandpa . . . and please, God, take care of yourself, or else we're all sunk!"

PREACH

First preacher: I think a pastor needs to study diligently for his Sunday morning message.

Second preacher: I disagree. Many times I have no idea what I am going to preach about but I go into the pulpit and preach and think nothing of it.

First preacher: And you are quite right in thinking nothing of it. Your deacons have told me they share your opinion.

⌘

Pastor: How did the assistant pastor do Sunday morning?

Member: It was a poor sermon. Nothing in it at all.

(Upon seeing the assistant pastor, the following conversation took place.)

Pastor: How did it go Sunday morning?

Assistant: Excellent. I didn't have time to prepare anything myself, so I preached one of your sermons.

∞——∞

A preacher once asked an actor why he had such large audiences and he, the preacher, had only a small audience at church.

"I act as if I believe in what I say," said the actor, "while you preach as if you did not believe what you preached."

∞——∞

Heckler: If I ever had a son who was a fool I'd make a preacher out of him.

Preacher: How come your father didn't send you to seminary?

∞——∞

Visitor: Your preacher is sure long-winded.

Member: He may be long . . . but never winded.

∞——∞

During a Christmas play: Not a preacher was stirring, not even a mouse.

∞——∞

America still has more marriages than divorces, proving that preachers can still outtalk lawyers.

∞——∞

"I am thankful that the Lord has opened my mouth to preach without my learning," said an illiterate preacher.

"A similar event took place in Balaam's time," replied a gentleman present.

◦◦—◦◦

Notice in the local newspaper of a small town: "In the future the preacher for next Sunday will be found hanging on the bulletin board."

Precinct

Sunk before you could get there.

Pregnant

An obviously pregnant woman and her husband were sitting in the obstetrician's waiting room. The wife looked at a lamp and commented on how lovely it was. Her husband gave her an anguished look and wailed, "Don't tell me you're starting to crave furniture!"

◦◦—◦◦

The rather awkward freshman at a prom finally got up enough nerve to ask a sultry young beauty for a dance. "I never dance with a child," said the pretty little snob.

The freshman looked her over critically and said, "Please forgive me; I didn't realize you were pregnant."

Prejudice

I think prejudice is a great time-saver. It helps us form our opinions without bothering to get the facts.

President

When I was a boy, I was told anybody could become president. I'm now beginning to believe it!

◦◦—◦◦

Pity poor old George Washington. He couldn't blame his troubles on the previous administration.

❦

A man walked up to the desk of a resort hotel and asked for a room.

"Have you a reservation?" asked the indifferent clerk.

"No. But I've been coming here every year for twelve years, and I've never had to have a reservation."

"Well, there is nothing available. We are filled up, and without a reservation you can't get a room."

"Suppose the president of the United States came in. You would have a room for him, wouldn't you?"

"Of course, for the president we would find a room—we would have a room."

"All right," said the man. "Now I'm telling you that the president isn't coming here tonight. So give me his room."

PROCRASTINATOR

Is it true that a procrastinator is a man with a wait problem?

PROFESSOR

A textbook wired for sound.

❦

One who talks in someone else's sleep.

❦

First student: What do they call old professor Jones?

Second student: They call him Sanka.

First student: Why do they call him that?

Second student: Because more than 98 percent of the active portion of the bean has been removed.

PROPHETS

First Roman (at Christian massacre): We've got a capacity crowd, but still we're losing money. The upkeep on the lions must be pretty heavy.
Second Roman: Yes, sir, these lions sure do eat the prophets.

PROPOSAL

Wife: Do you remember the night you proposed to me?
Husband: Yes.
Wife: I was silent for a whole hour after.
Husband: That was the happiest hour of my life.

❧——☙

"Jim proposed to me last night."
"Doesn't he do it nicely?"

❧——☙

"I've been asked to get married lots of times."
"Who asked you?"
"Mother and Father."

❧——☙

He: Will you marry me?
She: No.
And they lived happily ever after!

PROSPERITY

Something you feel, fold, and forward to Washington.

❧——☙

The sweet buy and buy.

PROVERB

Ozark proverb: Terrible is the fate to have a rooster who is silent and a hen who crows.

⌒⊙—⊙⌒

Cheerfulness is the window cleaner of the mind.

⌒⊙—⊙⌒

When life hands you a lemon, make lemonade.

PSYCHIATRIST

Patient: Every night when I get into bed I think that someone is under my bed. I then get up and look. There is never anyone there. When I crawl under the bed and lie down, I get the idea that there is someone on top of the bed. I then get up and look and I never find anyone on top of the bed. This goes on all night, up and down, up and down; it's driving me out of my mind. Do you think you can help?

Psychiatrist: I think I can. All you have to do is visit me twice a week for the next two years and I think I can cure you. The visits will cost seventy-five dollars an hour.

Patient: That is an awful lot of money for a working man like me. I'll have to talk it over with my wife and let you know.

The next week the patient phoned the psychiatrist.

Patient: I won't be back, doc. My wife solved the problem. She cut the legs off the bed.

⌒⊙—⊙⌒

"I have been coming to your counseling sessions for two years and all you do is listen to what I have to say. You never say anything back. I didn't have to go to a psychiatrist for that. I could have stayed home with my husband. That's all he does, too."

⌒⊙—⊙⌒

A man walked into a doctor's office with a pelican on his head.

"You need help immediately," said the doctor.

"I certainly do," said the pelican. "Get this man out from under me."

❧

A big-game hunter recently returned from Africa and went to a psychiatrist. He told the psychiatrist he didn't want to go through analysis, but would pay him two hundred dollars for answering two questions. The psychiatrist said this was highly irregular, but he agreed to do it.

"Is it possible," the hunter asked, "for a man to be in love with an elephant?"

The psychiatrist said, "Absolutely impossible. In all the annals of medicine, I've never heard of it. The whole idea is ridiculous. What's your second question?"

The man then asked meekly, "Do you know anyone who wants to buy a very large engagement ring?"

❧

Two psychiatrists met in the street. One of them kept brushing his jacket.

"What's new?" asked one.

"Nothing, really, only I have these invisible insects crawling on me!"

"Well," said the other, jumping back, "don't brush them off on me!"

❧

Psychiatrist: Now, will you be able to pay this bill for the counseling I've given you?

Patient: Don't worry. Don't worry, doc. You'll get the money or my name isn't King Henry VIII.

❧

A mother visiting a department store took her son to the toy department. Spying a gigantic rocking horse he climbed up on it and rocked back and forth for almost an hour.

"Come on, son," the mother pleaded. "I have to get home to get your father's dinner."

The little lad refused to budge and all her efforts were unavailing. The department manager also tried to coax the little fellow without meeting with any success. Eventually, in desperation they called the store's psychiatrist. Gently he walked over and whispered a few words in the boy's ear and immediately the lad jumped off and ran to his mother's side.

"How did you do it?" the mother asked incredulously. "What did you say to him?"

The psychiatrist hesitated for a moment, then said, "All I said was, 'If you don't jump off that rocking horse at once, son, I'll knock the stuffing out of you!'"

❦

Wife: My husband thinks he's a refrigerator.
Psychiatrist: I wouldn't worry as long as he is not violent.
Wife: Oh, the delusion doesn't bother me. But when he sleeps with his mouth open, the little light keeps me awake.

❦

Wife: My husband frightens me the way he blows smoke rings through his nose.
Psychiatrist: That isn't unusual.
Wife: But my husband doesn't smoke.

❦

Neurotics build air castles. Psychotics live in them. Psychiatrists collect the rent.

❦

Anyone who goes to a psychiatrist ought to have his head examined!

❦

Patient: I'm worried—I keep thinking I'm a pair of curtains.
Psychiatrist: Stop worrying and try to pull yourself together.

❦

My psychiatrist told me he knows what makes me tick, but he can't explain what makes me chime on the hours.

❦

Patient: I always feel that I'm covered in gold paint, doctor.
Psychiatrist: Oh, that's just your gilt complex.

❦

Roger: I used to think I was a beagle. But the psychiatrist cured me.
Dodger: How are you now?
Roger: Great. Just feel my nose.

❦

My son is really growing up. Only last week he was able to go to the psychiatrist all by himself.

❦

Patient: Doctor, I think everyone tries to take advantage of me.
Psychiatrist: That's silly. It's a perfectly normal feeling.
Patient: Is it really? Thanks for your help, doctor. How much do I owe you?
Psychiatrist: How much do you have?

❦

Patient (on phone): Doctor: I've decided to kill myself.
Psychiatrist: Don't do anything rash until you answer one question for me.
Patient: What's that?
Psychiatrist: Is your bill paid?

Psychologist

A man who, when a good-looking girl enters the room, looks at everybody else.

⁘—⁘

A high school student wrote: "I would like to be a psychologist. I plan on taking as much psychology as possible in college and maybe someday emerge another Fraud."

Pun

A form of humor that causes everyone to groan and is meant to punish the hearers.

Punishment

Wife: Tomorrow is our twenty-fifth anniversary. I think I'll kill the big red rooster and bake him.
Husband: Now, now, honey; why punish the poor chicken for what happened twenty-five years ago?

⁘—⁘

Husband: Listen to this. This article states that in some of the old Roman prisons that have been unearthed, they found the petrified remains of the prisoners.
Wife: Gracious! Those must be what they call hardened criminals.

⁘—⁘

A young businessman returned home after a tough day at the office and found his two daughters, both of about kindergarten age, acting up pretty boisterously. He gave them a moderately severe scolding and sent them off to bed. The next morning he found a note stuck on his bedroom door: "Be good to your children and they will be good to you. God."

Puppy Love

The beginning of a dog's life.

Push

Mother: Did you push your little sister down the stairs?
Bobby: I only pushed her down one step. She fell the rest of the way.

⇥ Q ⇤

QUACK

A doctor who ducks the law.

⚬——⚬

A quack was selling an elixir which he declared would make men live to a great age.

"Look at me," he shouted. "Hale and hearty. I'm over three hundred years old."

"Is he really as old as that?" asked a listener of the youthful assistant.

"I can't say," replied the assistant. "I've only worked for him for ninety-seven years."

QUARREL

Never pick a quarrel even when it's ripe.

QUESTIONS AND ANSWERS

Q: Where do armies live?
A: Up the sleevies of your jacket.

⚬——⚬

Q: What's a nun's favorite song?
A: I Left My Heart with San Franciscans.

⚬——⚬

Q: What's the best way to defeat your opponent?
A: Cut off his legs.

⚬——⚬

Q: What do they call a handsome, intelligent man in New York?
A: A tourist.

⚬⊸——⊶⚬

Q: What do you get if you cross a chicken with cement?
A: A bricklayer.

⚬⊸——⊶⚬

Q: What vegetable keeps the best musical rhythm?
A: The sugar beet.

⚬⊸——⊶⚬

Q: Which fly makes films?
A: Steven Spielbug.

⚬⊸——⊶⚬

Q: How do you make a glowworm happy?
A: Cut off its tail. It'll be delighted.

⚬⊸——⊶⚬

Q: What is sticky and plays the trumpet?
A: Gluey Armstrong.

⚬⊸——⊶⚬

Q: What did the German clock maker say to the broken clock?
A: Ve have vays of making you tock.

⚬⊸——⊶⚬

Q: What did the man do after his cat was run over by a steamroller?
A: He just sat there with a long puss.

⚬⊸——⊶⚬

Q: How do you avoid falling hair?
A: Jump out of the way.

Q: You load sixteen tons and what do you get?
A: A hernia!

Q: Name six animals that inhabit the Arctic region.
A: Three seals and three polar bears.

Q: Which month has twenty-eight days?
A: They all have.

Q: What goes woof, woof, tock?
A: A watchdog.

Q: How do you fix a broken tomato?
A: With tomato paste.

Q: What do cryogenicists sing when interring each new subject?
A: Freeze a Jolly Good Fellow.

Q: What's purple and surrounded by water?
A: Grape Britain.

Q: Why did the fig go out with a prune?
A: It couldn't find another date.

⟠—⟠

Q: What do you call two fat men having a chat?
A: A heavy discussion.

⟠—⟠

Q: What lies on the ground one hundred feet in the air?
A: A sunbathing centipede.

⟠—⟠

Q: How did Moses part the Red Sea?
A: With a sea saw.

⟠—⟠

Q: What do you call great bodies of water filled with grape juice?
A: The Grape Lakes.

⟠—⟠

Q: What ballet do squirrels like?
A: The Nutcracker.

⟠—⟠

Q: What's a pig's favorite ballet?
A: Swine Lake.

⟠—⟠

Q: What do you get when you cross peanut butter with an elephant?
A: You either get peanut butter that never forgets or an elephant that
sticks to the roof of your mouth.

⟠—⟠

Q: Why do elephants have wrinkles?
A: Have you ever tried to iron one?

Q: What do they call a bull that sleeps a lot?
A: A bulldozer.

Q: How many dead people are there in a cemetery?
A: All of them.

Q: What did one ear say to the other?
A: I didn't know we lived on the same block.

Q: Why did they make the fingers on the Statue of Liberty only eleven inches long?
A: One inch longer and it would have been a foot.

Q: How do you make anti-freeze?
A: Steal her blanket.

Q: April showers bring May flowers, but what do May flowers bring?
A: Pilgrims.

Q: What does an elephant do when he hurts his toe?
A: He calls a tow truck.

Q: Do you know what happened when they crossed an abalone with a crocodile?
A: A crock-a-baloney!

❧——☙

Q: Do you know what they got when they crossed a gorilla with a porcupine?
A: I don't know what you call it but it sure gets a seat on the subway!

❧——☙

Q: Do you know what they got when they crossed a rattlesnake with a horse?
A: I don't know what you call it, but if it bites you you can ride it to the hospital!

❧——☙

Q: What is the name of that lady with the wooden leg?
A: Peg!

❧——☙

Q: What is practical nursing?
A: Falling in love with a rich patient.

QUIET

A patient in a mental hospital placed his ear to the wall of his room, listening intently.

"Quiet," he whispered to an orderly and pointed to the wall.

The attendant pressed his ear against the wall, listened, and then said, "I don't hear anything."

"I know," replied the patient. "It's awful; it's been this way for days."

QUITTING

"My boss was sorry when I told him I was quitting next week."
"He was probably hoping it was this week."

QUOTABLE QUOTES

Why doesn't the fellow who says, "I'm no speechmaker," let it go at that, instead of giving a demonstration?

꙰—꙰

Many can rise to the occasion, but few know when to sit down.

꙰—꙰

When it comes to spreading gossip, the female of the species is much faster than the mail.

꙰—꙰

Two feet on the ground are worth one in the mouth.

꙰—꙰

Thrift is a wonderful virtue—especially in ancestors.

꙰—꙰

While money isn't everything in life, it does keep you in touch with your children.

꙰—꙰

The years that a woman subtracts from her age are not lost. They are added to the ages of other women.

꙰—꙰

Still, if nobody dropped out at the eighth grade, who would hire the college graduates?

꙰—꙰

To find out a girl's faults, praise her to her girlfriends.

꙰—꙰

Women's styles may change, but their designs remain the same.

⊰ R ⊱

Rabbit's Foot

First husband: I carry a rabbit's foot in my pocket because it saves me lots of money.

Second husband: How is that?

First husband: Every time my wife sticks her hand in my pocket she thinks it's a mouse.

Radio

Man has conquered the air but so has our neighbor's radio.

⸻

Pete: Do you know who owned the smallest radio in the world?

Bill: No, who?

Pete: Paul Revere—he broadcast from one plug.

Rain

"Is it raining outside?"

"Did you ever see it raining inside?"

Rainbow Tie

"That's a beautiful rainbow tie you are wearing!"

"What do you mean by a 'rainbow tie'?"

"It has a big pot at the end!"

RAISE

Employee: I have been here eleven years doing three men's work for one man's pay. Now I want a raise.

Boss: Well, I can't give you a raise but if you'll tell me who the other two men are, I'll fire them.

❧ — ❧

Worker: Boss, I came to see if you could raise my salary.

Boss: Relax and don't worry. I've managed to raise it each payday so far, haven't I?

❧ — ❧

New employee to boss: Well, if I can't have a raise, how about the same pay more often?

RAISIN BREAD

"Do you like raisin bread?"

"Don't know, I never tried raisin' any."

RAMPART

Paintings displayed on a ramp.

RATS

"I saw a big rat in my cookstove and when I went for my revolver, he ran out."

"Did you shoot him?"

"No. He was out of my range."

Raving Beauty

A girl who came out last in a beauty contest.

Razor-Blade Theme Song

"Nobody Knows the Stubble I've Seen"

Real Estate Agent

The first man to make a mountain out of a molehill was probably a real estate agent.

Realism

Artist: This is my latest painting. It is called Builders at Work. It is a piece of realism.
Customer: But I don't see any of the men at work.
Artist: Of course not—that is the realism part of it.

Reaping

The chaplain was passing through the prison garment factory. "Sewing?" he said to a prisoner who was at work. "No, chaplain," replied the prisoner gloomily, "reaping!"

Recession

Who is afraid of the recession? I've failed during boom times.

Recount

A recount is when the chairman can't believe his ayes.

RED CROSS

Despite warnings from his guide, an American skiing in Switzerland got separated from his group and fell—uninjured—into a deep crevasse. Several hours later, a rescue party found the yawning pit, and to reassure the stranded skier, shouted down to him, "We're from the Red Cross."

"Sorry," the imperturbable American echoed back, "I already gave at the office!"

REDSKINS

People on the American bathing beaches.

REDUCING DIET

Monday
Breakfast—Weak tea
Lunch—1 bouillon cube in 1/2 cup diluted water
Dinner—1 pigeon thigh & 2 oz. prune juice (gargle only)

Tuesday
Breakfast—Scraped crumbs from burned toast
Lunch—a doughnut hole (without sugar)
Dinner—2 jellyfish skins & 1 glass dehydrated water

Wednesday
Breakfast—Boiled-out stains from table cover
Lunch—1/2 doz. poppy seeds
Dinner—Bees knees & mosquito knuckles sauteed with vinegar

Thursday
Breakfast—Shredded eggshell skins
Lunch—Bellybutton from a navel orange
Dinner—3 eyes from Irish potatoes (diced)

Friday

Breakfast—2 lobster antennae
Lunch—1 guppy fin
Dinner—Jellyfish vertebrae à la Bookbinders

Saturday

Breakfast—4 chopped banana seeds
Lunch—Broiled butterfly liver
Dinner—Fillet of soft-shell crab slaw

Sunday

Breakfast—Pickled hummingbird tongue
Lunch—Prime ribs of tadpole and aroma of empty custard pie plate
Dinner—Tossed paprika & clover leaf (1) salad

NOTE: All meals to be eaten under microscope to avoid extra portion.

REFORM

Nothing so needs reforming as other people's habits.
—*Mark Twain*

REJECTION

There's a certain something about him that attracts women to other men.

RELATIVITY

When you are with a pretty girl for three hours, and it seems like only three minutes; and then you sit on a hot stove for a minute and think it's an hour.

RELIEF

My small son approached me the other day and asked if there was anything he could do around the house to earn a little pocket money.

"I can't think of anything."
"Well, then, will you put me on relief?"

❦

Tom: Every time I pass a girl she sighs.
Jerry: With relief.

REMARRIAGE

The triumph of hope over existence.

RENO

A large inland seaport in America with the tide running in and other untied running out.

❦

Where the honeymoon express is finally uncoupled.

REPARTEE

An insult with a college education.

❦

Something great we think of twenty-four hours too late.

REPLACEMENT

Employee: Say, boss, your assistant just died, and I was wondering if I could take his place?
Boss: It's all right with me if you can arrange it with the undertaker.

Reporter

A brand-new reporter was sent out by the editor to cover the story of a man who could sing opera without interruption while he was eating a seven-course meal.

The reporter came back and did not write up the story.

The editor wanted to know the details.

"Oh, there was not much to it. The guy had two heads."

Reproach

To remind a man of the good turns you have done him is very much like a reproach.

—Demosthenes

Resolution

Good resolutions are simply checks that men draw on a bank where they have no account.

—Oscar Wilde

Responsible

Employer: We want a responsible man for this job.

Applicant: Well, I guess I'm your man. In all the other jobs I have worked at, whenever anything went wrong, they told me I was responsible.

Restaurant

An institution for the distribution of indigestion.

Man in restaurant: I'll have the five-dollar dinner.
Waitress: Would you like that on white or dark bread?

⌒◦—◦⌒

Restaurant chains: Cook-alikes.

RETORT

A very thin man met a very fat man in the hotel lobby.
"From the looks of you," said the fat man, "there might have been a famine."
"Yes," was the reply, "and from the looks of you, you might have caused it."

⌒◦—◦⌒

A speaker was having a little trouble getting started in his speech. All of a sudden someone from the audience shouted: "Tell 'em all you know. It will only take a minute."
"I'll tell 'em all we both know," shot back the speaker. "It won't take any longer."

⌒◦—◦⌒

"Darling, I read your new book yesterday. I loved it. Who wrote it for you?"
"I'm glad you liked it. Who read it to you?"

⌒◦—◦⌒

"Oh, Sarah, I completely forgot about your little party last night."
"Weren't you there?"

RETROACTIVE

This letter-to-the-editor appeared in a local newspaper: I have read recently that the word "obey" is now being omitted from the wedding ceremony. May I ask if you think the new wording for the wedding service is retroactive?

RETURNED CHECK

Husband: The bank returned the check you wrote.
Wife: Good. What shall we buy with it this time?

REVENUE

Internal Revenue man, eyeing taxpayer's expense claims: Shall we go over this item by item or would you prefer to chicken out right now?

RHUBARB

Bloodshot celery.

RICH

Beverly: A scientist says that what we eat we become.
Melba: Oh, boy, let's order something rich.

∾᳐ᴇ᠊

Better to live rich than to die rich.

RICH RELATIVES

The kin we love to touch.

∾᳐ᴇ᠊

Q: What type of person lives the longest?
A: A rich relative.

RIDICULOUS

Wife: I got this girdle today for a ridiculous figure.
Husband: I know. But how much did it cost?

THE RIGHT ROW

A man and his wife were running to their seats after a movie intermission. In a voice of concern, he asked a man at the end of a row, "Did I step on your toes on the way out?"

"You certainly did," responded the other angrily.

"All right," he said, turning to his wife. "This is our row."

RIGHTEOUS INDIGNATION

Righteous indignation is your own wrath as opposed to the shocking bad temper of others.

ROBERT E. LEE

A man from the deep South was about to jump from the window of a building when a passerby saw him and tried to talk him out of it. "For the sake of your mother, don't do it!" the passerby pleaded.

"I don't have a mother."

"Well, think of your father."

"I don't have a father."

"Well, think of your wife."

"I never married."

"Well, then, think of Robert E. Lee!"

"Robert E. Lee? Who's he?"

"Never mind, Yankee. Go ahead and jump!"

ROCK BOTTOM

A rocking chair.

ROCK 'N' ROLL

I guess you read about the rock 'n' roll show that turned into a riot. What bothers me is, how could they tell?

⌒⊙—⊙⌒

Advertisement in newspaper: For sale cheap . . . my son's collection of rock 'n' roll records. If a boy's voice answers the phone, hang up and call later.

ROMEO AND JULIET

Man: I'm sorry I can't come to your party tonight. I have an engagement to see Romeo and Juliet.
Woman: That's all right. Bring them along, too.

ROOSTER

Q: Why did the boy name his rooster Robinson?
A: Because it Crusoe.

ROPE

"Did you ever hear the rope joke?"
"No."
"Skip it."

ROUGH NEIGHBORHOOD

I lived in such a rough neighborhood as a child that my mom would give me a dollar each morning for the holdup man.

Rubber Band

Kathy: Did anyone around here lose a roll of bills with a rubber band?
Stan: Yes, I did.
Kathy: Well, I've found the rubber band.

Rudolph

Mr. and Mrs. Smith were touring Russia. Their guide's name was Rudolph. Mr. Smith and Rudolph argued all the time. As the couple was leaving Moscow, the husband said, "Look, it's snowing out."
The guide disagreed. "No, sir, it's raining out."
"I still think it's snowing," said Mr. Smith.
But his wife replied, "Rudolph the Red knows rain, dear."

Rumor

A rumor goes in one ear and out many mouths.

⚬⎯⚬

Rumor is one thing that gets thicker as you spread it.

⚬⎯⚬

There is no such thing as an idle rumor.

Run

Recent studies reveal that city-dwellers do not walk for their health—they run.

Russians

First Russian prisoner: What are you in for?
Second prisoner: I came to work late. How about you?

First prisoner: I came to work early, so they arrested me on suspicion.

Third prisoner: Well, I'm here because I arrived at work exactly on time.

Second prisoner: What kind of offense is that?

Third prisoner: They said I must own an American watch.

⟡

If we're lucky the Russians will steal some of our secrets, and then they'll be two years behind us.

⟡

"Did you hear that the Russian chess champion died after he lost the game to an American?"

"When did that happen?"

"Tomorrow."

❈ S ❈

SALESMAN

Sales manager: Did you get any orders today?
Salesman: Yes, I got two orders.
Sales manager: What for?
Salesman: One to get out and the other to stay out.

❧—❧

Salesman one: I made some very valuable contacts today.
Salesman two: I didn't make any sales, either.

❧—❧

Door-to-door salesman: Are your parents in, little girl?
Little girl: They was, but they's out now.
Salesman: Tsk, tsk. Where's your grammar?
Little girl: She's in the kitchen baking bread.

❧—❧

Angry customer: I thought you said this was a good car. It won't even go uphill.
Used car dealer: I said, "On the level, it's a fine car."

SANTA CLAUS

Mother: Well, Lisa, did you see Santa Claus last night?
Lisa: No. It was too dark to see him, but I heard what he said when he stubbed his toe against the chair in the living room.

❧—❧

Elmer: Mother, where did all these pretty toys come from?

Mother: Why, dear, Santa brought them.

Elmer: Did he bring everything? Did he bring the electric train, the baseball glove, the ice skates . . .

Mother: Yes, he brought everything.

Elmer: Well, who buys all the things in the stores?

❦

Did you hear about the man who went behind the barn the night before Christmas, fired a shot, and then told his two children Santa Claus had committed suicide?

SAXOPHONE

"Would you donate five dollars to bury a saxophone player?"

"Here's thirty dollars; bury six of them."

SCHOOL DAYS

School days are the best days of your life . . . provided your children are old enough to go.

❦

One young mother, on receiving a nursery school report that described her daughter as "emotionally immature," asked with good sense, "If you can't be immature at three, when can you be?"

❦

The mother was having a hard time getting her son to go to school in the morning.

"Nobody in school likes me," he complained. "The teachers don't like me, the kids don't like me, the superintendent wants to transfer me, the bus drivers hate me, the school board wants me to drop out, and the custodians have it in for me. I don't want to go to school."

"But you have to go to school," countered his mother. "You are healthy, you have a lot to learn, you have something to offer others, you are a leader. And besides, you are forty-five years old and you are the principal."

∽⊖—ℓ∾

Teacher: What are you—animal, vegetable, or mineral?
Little boy: Vegetable. I am a human bean!

∽⊖—ℓ∾

Son to father: Remember, you promised me twenty dollars if I passed math. Well, I've got great news. You've just saved twenty dollars.

∽⊖—ℓ∾

Teacher: Children, we can learn from the ants. Ants work very hard every day. The ant works all the time. And what happens in the end?
Student: Somebody steps on him.

∽⊖—ℓ∾

Teacher: You can be sure that if Moses were alive today, he'd be considered a remarkable man.
Lenny: He sure ought to be—he'd be more than 2,500 years old.

∽⊖—ℓ∾

It was the little girl's first day at school and the teacher was making out her registration card.
"What is your father's name?"
"Daddy," replied the child.
"Yes, I know, but what does your mother call him?"
"Oh, she doesn't call him anything. She likes him!"

∽⊖—ℓ∾

Student: I'm very tired. I was up till midnight doing my homework.
Teacher: What time did you begin?
Student: Eleven fifty-five.

∾—᷒

Student: Would you punish someone for something they didn't do?
Teacher: Of course not.
Student: Good, 'cause I haven't done my homework.

∾—᷒

"Some plants," said the teacher, "have the prefix 'dog.' For instance, there is the dogrose, the dogwood, the dogviolet. Who can name another plant prefixed by 'dog?'"
"I can," shouted a little boy in the back row. "Collie flower."

∾—᷒

A student wrote the following on his pre-Christmas examination paper: "God only knows the answer to this question. Merry Christmas!"
The professor returned the paper with the following notation: "God gets an 'A'; you get an 'F'. Happy New Year!"

∾—᷒

The quickest way for a child to get attention in school these days is for him to bend his IBM card.

∾—᷒

Father: I hope you're not talking in class anymore!
Son: Not any more . . . just about the same amount.

∾—᷒

Father: What did you learn in school today, Clarence?
Clarence: How to whisper without moving my lips.

∾—᷒

Father: Well, son, what did you learn in school today?
Son: I learned to say, "Yes, sir," and "No, sir," and "No, ma'am," and "Yes, ma'am."
Father: Really?
Son: Yeah!

❦

Teacher: Billy, you've got your shoes on the wrong feet.
Billy: They're the only feet I have.

❦

Teacher: If I write n-e-w on the blackboard, what does it spell?
Student: New.
Teacher: Now, I'll put a "k" in front of it and what do we have?
Student: Canoe.

Scotchman

A Scotchman fell down a well. The water was way over his head and icy cold, but he could swim. He kept himself afloat and called out until his wife came to the edge of the well.

"I can't do a thing," she called down. "Just try to keep your head up and I'll call the men in from the field to pull you out."

"What time is it?"

"A little before eleven o'clock," she said.

"Well, don't ring for the boys now. Let them work until lunch time. I'll swim around till then."

❦

Did you hear about the Scotchman who counted his money in front of the mirror so he wouldn't cheat himself?

Scratch Paper

Stu: I guess my pen will just have to go on itching.

Sue: Why?

Stu: I'm all out of scratch paper.

Sermon

Rocking horse sermon—back and forth, back and forth, but going nowhere.

Mockingbird sermon—repetition, nothing new.

Smorgasbord sermon—a little bit of everything, but nothing solid.

Jericho sermon—march around the subject seven times.

Christmas tree sermon—something offered for nothing.

❦

The sermon was very long this Sunday morning and little Donny was getting more restless by the minute.

Suddenly, in a whisper too loud for his mother's comfort, he blurted out, "If we give him the money now, Ma, will he let us go out?"

❦

"I think we need to change the morning hymn," said the minister to his song leader. "My topic this morning is 'gossip.' I don't think 'I Love to Tell the Story' would be the best song."

❦

A little boy in church, awaking after a nap, asked his father, "Has the preacher finished?"

"Yes, Son, he has finished, but he hasn't stopped."

❦

A minister went to visit some members of his church who owned a small farm. Before leaving for the morning service, the members invited him for breakfast. He declined saying that he found he did not preach well following a hearty meal.

When the members returned home after the morning services, the wife said to the husband, "He might as well have eaten."

⁓⊖⊸

Member to pastor at the end of the morning service: Pastor, you were really good this morning! You interrupted my thoughts at least half a dozen times!

⁓⊖⊸

Clara: My pastor is so good he can talk on any subject for an hour.
Sarah: That's nothing! My pastor can talk for an hour without a subject!

Ship

The first mate on a ship got drunk for the first time in his life. The ship's captain, a stern and rigid man, recorded in his log, "The first mate got drunk today."

The mate protested against the entry, explaining that if it remained in the log without further comment or explanation it could ruin his career because it suggested that drunkenness was not unusual for him, whereas he had never been drunk before. The captain, however, was adamant, stating that the log recorded the exact truth and therefore must stand as written.

The next week it was the mate's turn to write the ship's log. And on each day he wrote, "The Captain was sober today."

⁓⊖⊸

"Shall I bring you lunch on deck, sir?"
"Just throw it overboard and save time."

Shoe Repair

While rummaging through his attic, a man found a shoe-repair ticket that was nine years old. Figuring that he had nothing to lose, he went to the shop and presented the ticket to the proprietor, who reluctantly began a search for the unclaimed shoes. After ten minutes, the owner reappeared and handed back the ticket.

"Well," asked the customer, "did you find the pair?"
"Yes," replied the shop owner. "They'll be ready Tuesday."

SHOT

"Oh! Oh! I'm hit!"
"You shot bad, Tex?"
"You ever hear of anyone being shot good?"

SIGNS OF THE TIMES

FREE! FREE!
One shoe shined absolutely free.

❦

On the desk of a kindergarten teacher:
THINK SMALL

❦

Pawnshop sign:
PLEASE SEE ME AT YOUR EARLIEST INCONVENIENCE.

❦

Sign in office:
THE EASIEST WAY TO MAKE ENDS MEET IS TO GET OFF YOUR OWN.

❦

Sign at butcher shop:
HONEST SCALES—NO TWO WEIGHS ABOUT IT.

❦

Sign by stuffed fish on the wall:
IF I HAD KEPT MY MOUTH SHUT I WOULDN'T BE HERE.

❦

Sign on travel agency window:
PLEASE GO AWAY!

❦

Sign in undertaker's window:
DRIVE CAREFULLY—WE CAN WAIT.

❦

Sign at cafe:
EAT HERE AND YOU'LL NEVER EAT ANYPLACE ELSE AGAIN!

❦

Sign in restaurant:
OUR CUSTOMERS ARE ALWAYS RIGHT: MISIN-FORMED, PERHAPS, INEXACT, BULLHEADED, FICKLE, EVEN DOWNRIGHT STUPID, BUT NEVER WRONG.

SINGING

Kathy: My husband is just the opposite of me. While I sing he grumbles and growls.

Nancy: Then why don't you stop singing?

❦

The choir soloist was practicing in the church with all the windows open. When she stepped outside for a breath of fresh air, she noticed the gardener working in the flower bed. "How did you like my execution?" the soloist asked.

The gardener looked up and said, "I'm in favor of it."

❦

Son: Why is father singing to the baby so much tonight?
Mother: He is trying to sing her to sleep.
Son: Well, if I were her, I'd pretend I was asleep.

∽⎯e∾

"I spent over $100,000 on voice lessons, learning to sing."
"I would love for you to meet my brother."
"Is he a singer, too?"
"No, he's a lawyer. He might be able to get your money back."

SLOWLY

Mr. and Mrs. McKee, vacationing in Rome, were being shown through the Colosseum.
"Now, this room," said the guide, "is where the slaves dressed to fight the lions."
"But how does one dress to fight lions?" inquired Mr. McKee.
"Very slow-w-w-w-w-wly," replied the guide.

SMALL HUMOR

Q: How do you milk an ant?
A: First, you get a low stool . . .

SMOGARIA

The country of Smogaria is a neutral country. Smogarians are about as dumb as they come. They really need help! In fact, their library only has one book in it, their national bird is the fly, and in their last beauty pageant, nobody won. When asked how many Smogarians it takes to screw a light bulb, they responded, "What's a light bulb?"

∽⎯e∾

Two Smogarians were dragging a deer through the woods by its tail when they ran across another hunter. "It would be easier," said the hunter, "if you would drag the deer by the antlers instead of the tail. Then he won't get caught on all the bushes."

The two Smogarians did as the hunter suggested. After about an hour of dragging the deer by the antlers, one Smogarian said to the other, "This is sure a lot easier."

"Yeah," said the second Smogarian, "but I think we are going in the wrong direction."

Q: Why is it impossible to walk across Smogaria?
A: Nobody can hold his nose for that long.

Q: Do you know why it takes a Smogarian five days to wash his basement windows?
A: He needs four and a half days to dig the holes for the ladder.

Did you hear about the Smogarian who went to the store for some birdseed?

"For which kind of bird?" asked the clerk.

"Oh, I dunno," replied the Smogarian. "Whichever kind will grow the fastest."

Three men were sitting around a table at a restaurant discussing the strides mankind has made in the twentieth century.

"If you ask me," said the first man, "the smartest invention of our time is the computer. Think of all the figuring and word processing it can do with just the press of a button."

The second man said, "The computer is great, but it is not as complicated as the cruise missile. Imagine being able to follow a target wherever it goes."

Shaking his head, the third man, a Smogarian, said, "You're both way off base. The smartest invention of the twentieth century is the thermos."

The other two men looked at him and said in unison, "The thermos?"

"You bet. It keeps hot things hot, and cold things cold. Now tell me: How does it know?"

❦

During the war, an Englishman, a Frenchman, and a Smogarian were captured by the Germans. Each man was sentenced to stand before a firing squad.

The Englishman was the first to be put against the wall. Standing back the Germans said, "Ready, aim . . ."

At which point the Englishman shouted, "Earthquake!"

The firing squad ran for cover, and the Englishman escaped.

Regrouping, the Germans put the Frenchman against the wall. Once again the Germans said, "Ready, aim . . ."

"Flood!" the Frenchman yelled.

Once again the Germans panicked, and the prisoner escaped.

Finally, the Smogarian faced the guns. But he was ready to use the same tactic that the Englishman and the Frenchman used.

The Germans said, "Ready, aim . . ."

"Fire!" hollered the Smogarian.

❦

Q: Why doesn't General Motors give their Smogarian mechanics a coffee break?

A: Takes too long to retrain them.

❦

Q: How many Smogarians does it take to change a light bulb?

A: Three. One to hold the bulb and two to turn the ladder.

❦

"Do you speak Smogarian?"

"No."

"Do you read Smogarian?"
"No."
"Do you write Smogarian?"
"No."
"Do you know how many Smogarians are in Smogaria?"
"No."
"How does it feel to be dumber than a Smogarian?"

***

A perfect gift for a Smogarian who has everything . . . a garbage truck to keep it in.

***

Did you know Smogarian dogs have flat noses? . . . from chasing parked cars.

***

Did you hear about the Smogarian race track driver at Indianapolis who came in last? His average speed was 6.49 m.p.h. He had to make seventy-five pit stops—three for fuel, two to have the tires changed, and seventy to ask for directions.

***

The most dangerous job in Smogaria . . . riding shotgun on a garbage truck.

***

Q: What's the capital of Smogaria?
A: About thirteen dollars.

***

Did you hear about the Smogarian beauty contest? Nobody won.

SMOKING

First smoker: I see that you smoke the same kind of cigarettes that I do.

Second smoker: Yes, but I don't save the coupons on the back. Do you?

First smoker: Of course. How do you think I got my artificial lung?

❦

Did you hear about the man who read that smoking was bad for your health? He immediately gave up reading.

❦

"Would you like a cigarette?"
"No, thank you. I think I already have cancer!"

❦

I don't smoke but I chew. Don't blow your smoke on me, and I won't spit on you.

SNORING

Why is it that the loudest snorer is always the first one to get to sleep?

SNOWFLAKE

Mankind should learn a lesson from the snowflake. No two of them are alike, and yet observe how well they cooperate on major projects, such as tying up traffic.

SOFT AND SWEET

Terry: Say something soft and sweet.
Jerry: Marshmallow.

SPEAKER

A manufacturer of bicycle tires was the speaker at a businessmen's luncheon. In response to a toast, he said, "I have no desire or intention to inflict upon you a long speech, for it is well known in our trade that the longer the spoke, the bigger the tire."

❦

Some speakers are good. Some speakers are lousy. Some are good and lousy.

❦

Seated next to a blowhard at a UN dinner was an Oriental fellow dressed in the robes of one of the Far Eastern countries.

The blowhard, attempting to make conversation, leaned over and said: "You like soupee?" The Oriental fellow nodded his head. "You like steakee?" The Oriental nodded again.

As it turned out, the guest speaker at the dinner was our Oriental friend, who got up and delivered a beautiful fifty-minute address on the UN definition of encouragement to self-reliance by underdeveloped countries of the world. The speech was in flawless Oxford English.

He returned to his place at the head of the table, sat down, turned to his dinner partner, and said, "You like speechee?"

❦

When he finally finished his speech, there was a great awakening.

❦

Speaker: This is terrible! I am the speaker at this banquet and I forgot my false teeth!
Man: I happen to have an extra pair; try these.
Speaker: Too small!
Man: Well, try this pair.
Speaker: Too big!
Man: I have one pair left.

Speaker: These fit just fine. It sure is lucky to sit next to a dentist!
Man: I'm not a dentist. I am an undertaker.

∽⊙—⊙∾

Only one man applauded; he was slapping his head to keep awake.

∽⊙—⊙∾

History repeats itself—and so does this guy!

∽⊙—⊙∾

The fault with many speakers is that you can't hear what they're saying. The trouble with this one is that you can.

∽⊙—⊙∾

I was a young fellow when this speech started!

∽⊙—⊙∾

During a long lecture a speaker suffered many interruptions from a man in the balcony who kept yelling: "Louder! Louder!"
After about the fifth interruption, a gentleman in the first row stood up, looked back, and said, "What's the matter, my friend, can't you hear?"
"No, I can't hear," came the answer from the balcony.
"Well, then, be thankful and shut up!"

∽⊙—⊙∾

The entire audience was hissing except one man. He was applauding the hissing.

∽⊙—⊙∾

A lecture is something that can make you feel numb at one end and dumb at the other.

∽⊙—⊙∾

"Did his speech have a happy ending?"

"Sure everybody was glad it was over."

∽——∾

At a banquet, several long-winded speakers covered almost every subject possible.

When yet another speaker rose, he said, "It seems to me everything has already been talked about. But if someone will tell me what to talk about, I will be grateful."

From the back of the room a voice shouted, "Talk about a minute!"

∽——∾

Did you hear about the wife of a speaker who took her husband's temperature with a barometer instead of a thermometer? It read Dry and Windy.

∽——∾

He's always offering "sound advice" . . . 99 percent sound and 1 percent advice.

∽——∾

He's suffering from I-strain.

∽——∾

He's an M.C. all right . . . a mental case.

∽——∾

He speaks straight from the shoulder. Too bad his remarks don't start from higher up.

∽——∾

Did you hear about the man who was speaking and someone in the audience went to sleep during his boring talk? He got so mad that he took the gavel and hit the sleeping man in the head. The sleeper woke up, took a long look at the speaker, and said, "Hit me again. I can still hear you."

＊ ＊

Every time he opens his mouth, he puts his feats in.

＊ ＊

He's an expert at handing out baloney disguised as food for thought.

＊ ＊

He reminds you of a bee—a humbug.

＊ ＊

He reminds you of a clarinet—a wind instrument.

＊ ＊

Our speaker has not only all of the five senses but he has two more, horse and common.

＊ ＊

He can wrap up a one-minute idea in a one-hour vocabulary.

＊ ＊

An inexperienced speaker arose in confusion after dinner and murmured stumblingly, "M-m-my f-f-friends, when I came here tonight, only God and myself knew what I was about to say to you . . . and now only God knows."

＊ ＊

"His last speech had the audience in the aisles."
"Applauding?"

"No, stretching and yawning."

∽⊙—⊙∾

If he said what he thought, he'd be speechless.

∽⊙—⊙∾

They call him the "Mastoid of Ceremonies"—he's a pain in the ear.

∽⊙—⊙∾

His wisecracks are always greeted with a tremendous burst of silence.

∽⊙—⊙∾

Every year he takes a boast-to-boast tour.

∽⊙—⊙∾

He holds people open-mouthed with his conversations. They can't stop yawning.

Specialist

A doctor whose patients are expected to confine their ailments to his office hours.

Speech

Wife: How was your talk tonight?
Husband: Which one?
Wife: What do you mean, which one?
Husband: The one I was going to give, the one I did give, or the one I delivered so brilliantly to myself on the way home in the car?

∽⊙—⊙∾

"That was a great speech, sir . . . I liked the straightforward way you dodged those issues."

SPEEDING

"I know about a motorist, going eighty, who tried to beat a speeding train to an intersection."

"Did the motorist get across?"

"He got a cross, all right . . . a beautiful marble cross purchased by his beneficiaries."

❧

He: My wife just got a ticket for speeding.

Him: That's nothing! My wife is so bad the police gave her a season ticket.

SPHINX

Professor: Jones, can you tell me who built the Sphinx?

Student: I-I-I did know, sir, but I've forgotten!

Professor: Great guns, what a calamity! The only man living who knows, and he has forgotten!

SPINACH

Mother: Robbie, eat your spinach. It's good for growing children.

Robbie: Who wants to grow children?

SPINSTER

The most singular of women.

❧

A woman who goes around and around looking for a man.

SPIRITUALIST

A trance-guesser.

SPOKESMAN

He who talks like a big wheel may be only a spokesman.

SPORTING

It was hunting season when a state trooper walked up to a man and his son, and said, "That's a nice buck you have on the top of your car." The surprised man couldn't say anything, so his son answered for him, "That's nothing! You should see the one we have in the trunk!"

Boxer: Have I done any damage?
Trainer: No, but keep swinging. The draft might give him a cold.

There are two kinds of hunters . . . those who hunt for sport and those who catch something.

Golfer: Pardon me, but would you mind if I played through? I've just heard that my wife has been taken seriously ill.

"When I was in India," said the club bore, "I saw a tiger come down to the water where some women were washing clothes. It was a very fierce tiger, but one woman, with great presence of mind, splashed some water in its face and it slunk away."

"Gentlemen," said a man in an armchair, "I can vouch for the truth of this story. Some minutes after this incident, I was coming down to the water. I met this tiger, and, as is my habit, stroked its whiskers. Gentlemen, those whiskers were wet."

⟨ဝ—ဝ⟩

Two boxers had placed bets and each backed himself to lose the fight. During the progress of the bout, one accidentally hit his opponent a light tap on the face. He immediately lay down and the referee proceeded to count him out. The other boxer was in a quandary. Just as the referee got to nine, he had a magnificent idea come to him. He rushed to the prostrate man and kicked him, and was instantly disqualified.

⟨ဝ—ဝ⟩

Two hunters had been out several hours and one of them had been growing uneasy. Finally panic overtook him. "We're lost!" he cried to his companion. "What shall we do?"

"Keep your shirt on!" said his companion. "Shoot an extra deer and the game warden will be here in a minute and a half."

⟨ဝ—ဝ⟩

Sportsman: Is there much good hunting in these parts?
Native: Sure, there's plenty of hunting but very little finding.

⟨ဝ—ဝ⟩

Talkative hunter: Once while I was having a meal in the jungle, a lion came so close to me that I could feel his breath on the back of my neck. What did I do?
Bored listener: Turned your collar up?

Sports Cars

One nice thing about small sports cars . . . if you flood the carburetor, you can just put the car over your shoulder and burp it.

❦

Sports car driver: Yes, my car is air-conditioned and it gets forty miles to an ice cube.

❦

This afternoon I saw two little cars under a station wagon. I didn't know if they were hiding or nursing.

Spouting Off

Be reminded of the whale: When it's spouting off, that is when it is in the most danger of being harpooned.

Springtime

On the first day of springtime my true love gave to me: five packs of seed, four sacks of fertilizer, three cans of weed killer, two bottles of insect spray, and a pruning knife for the pear tree.

Squeaks

Wife: George, wake up, there's a mouse in the bedroom. I can hear it squeaking.
Husband (as he rolled over): What do you want me to do? Get up and oil it?

Stages of Life

The seven ages of a woman are baby, child, girl, young woman, young woman, young woman, and poised social leader.

∽⊙—⊘∾

Three stages of man: Youth; Middle age; "You're looking fine."

∽⊙—⊘∾

The three stages of man: He believes in Santa Claus; he does not believe in Santa Claus; he is Santa Claus.

Start a Ripple

He has so many chins, he should be careful not to burp—it would start a ripple.

Station

A janitor who worked in a railroad station decided to get married in a huge room on the upper floor of the station. So many friends and kinfolk showed up, their combined weight caused the building to collapse. Moral of the story: Never marry above your station.

Statistics

Statistics prove that marriage is a preventive of suicide. But, on the other hand, they also prove that suicide is a preventive of marriage.

Steady

Bill: I'm a steady worker.
Bob: Yeah, and if you were any steadier, you would be motionless.

STEAM

Too many people work up a head of steam before they find out what's cooking.

৵৹—৹৵

Father: What good is the steam that comes out of the spout on the kettle when it boils?
Son: Mother can open your letter before you get home.

STEP ON IT

Customer: Waitress, why is my doughnut all smashed?
Waitress: You said you wanted a cup of coffee and a doughnut, and step on it.

STIRRUP

What you do with cake batter.

STOCKS

March is a very dangerous month in which to speculate in stocks. The other months are April, May, June, July, August, September, October, November, December, January, and February.

STONES

The following are famous birthstones:
For architects, the cornerstone.
For beauties, the peachstone.
For borrowers, the touchstone.
For burglars, the keystone.
For cooks, the puddingstone.

For editors, the grindstone.
For laundresses, the soapstone.
For motorists, the milestone.
For pedestrians, the tombstone.
For policemen, the pavingstone.
For politicians, the blarneystone.
For soldiers, the boldstone.
For stockbrokers, the curbstone.
For tourists, the Yellowstone.

STOP THE PRESSES

Newspaper misprint:
Mr. Carlson won a ten-pound turkey at Saturday's shurkey toot.

❦

Newspaper misprint:
At the Ladies' Aid Society meeting many interesting articles were raffled off. Every member brought something she no longer needed. Many members brought their husbands.

❦

Newspaper misprint:
First printing: Mr. Janelli was a defective in the police force.
Correction: Mr. Janelli was a detective in the police farce.

❦

Newspaper misprint:
The wildwife league will meet tonight.

❦

Church bulletin misprint:
Nine volunteers put in new church furnace.

❦

Newspaper misprint:
Father of ten shot—mistaken for rabbit.

❦

Newspaper misprint:
Dr. Jeremiah is the author of a brand-new book that is expected to outsmell the two million copies of his first book.

❦

Newspaper misprint:
Man found dead in cemetery.

❦

Newspaper misprint:
For sale: A full-blooded cow, giving three gallons of milk, two tons of hay, a lot of chickens, and a cookstove.

❦

Newspaper misprint:
The general will remain unequalled in history for his accomplishment on the bottlefield.

❦

Newspaper misprint:
Help Wanted: Adult or mature teenager to babysit. One dollar an hour, plus frige benefits.

STORK

The bird with the big bill.

STORY

We like the fellow who says he is going to make a long story short, and does.

STRIKE

One sit-down strike in a public building was ended very quickly. The official in charge of the building simply locked all the toilets.

∾⊖—⊖∾

"My uncle is still on strike."
"How long has he been on strike?"
"Fifty-two years."

∾⊖—⊖∾

One particular company was having a problem with all the employees going on a sit-down strike.

A very smart executive told the strikers that they might as well be comfortable, so he provided them with blankets and cases of brandy. When the brandy was half-consumed, the boss sent in ten young women to entertain the sit-downers. Then he brought over the strikers' wives so that they could see how comfortable their husbands were. That ended the sit-down strike.

STUDY

Why study? The more we know, the more we forget. The more we forget, the less we know. The less we know, the less we forget. The less we forget, the more we know. So why study?

STUPENDOUS

Advanced stupidity.

Submarine

First rookie: Did you volunteer for submarine service?
Second rookie: No, sir. I don't want to get on a ship that sinks on purpose.

Subsidy

A town underneath another town.

Succeed

If at first you don't succeed, you'll have a lot more friends.

Suffer

Some persons won't suffer in silence because that would take the pleasure out of it.

Sugar

Ben: One of our little pigs was sick so I gave him some sugar.
Dan: Sugar! What for?
Ben: Haven't you ever heard of sugar-cured ham?

Suicide

The last thing a person should do.

⚬—⚬

Frontier coroner's verdict: We find that the deceased came to his death by an act of suicide. At a distance of a hundred yards he opened fire with a six-shooter upon a man armed with a rifle.

Sunburn Oil

Husband: Why does this meat taste so funny?
Wife: Well, I burned it a little . . . but I put some sunburn oil on it at once.

Sunday School

Son: Dad, did you go to Sunday school when you were young?
Dad: Never missed a Sunday.
Son: Bet it won't do me any good either.

◦ↄ——ↄ◦

Sunday school teacher: What must you do to receive the forgiveness of sin?
Pupil: Sin.

◦ↄ——ↄ◦

Q: Who was Round John Virgin?
A: One of the twelve Opossums.

◦ↄ——ↄ◦

Sunday school teacher: Now, who decreed that all the world should be taxed?
Student: The Democrats.

◦ↄ——ↄ◦

Father: What did you learn in Sunday school this morning?
Son: We learned about how Moses went behind enemy lines to rescue the Jews from the Egyptians. Moses ordered the engineers to build a pontoon bridge. After the people crossed, he sent bombers back to blow up the bridge and the Egyptian tanks that were following them. And then . . .

Father: Did your teacher really tell it like that?
Son: No, but if I told you what he said you would never believe it!

∽⊖─⊖∼

A little boy came home from Sunday school and told his mother that they had just learned a new song about a boy named Andy. His mother couldn't understand what he meant until he sang:
Andy walks with me,
Andy talks with me,
Andy tells me I am His own. . . .

∽⊖─⊖∼

Overheard after Sunday school:
"Is it true that shepherds have dirty socks?"
"What do you mean?"
"I heard that the shepherds washed their socks by night."

∽⊖─⊖∼

Sunday school teacher: Why would it be wrong to cut off a cat's tail?
Student: The Bible says, "What God hath joined together, let no man put asunder."

∽⊖─⊖∼

A clergyman had been invited to attend a party of the Sunday school nursery department. He decided to surprise them, so getting on his hands and knees, flapping his coattails over his head like wings, he hopped in on all fours, cackling like a bird. Imagine his surprise when he learned that due to a switch in locations, he had intruded on the ladies' missionary meeting!

SUPERIOR

Son: Dad, do you think that the American Indians were superior to the white men who took this land from them?

Father: You bet. When the Indians were the sole occupants of this land, they had no taxes, no national debt, no centralized government, no military draft, no foreign-aid programs, no banks, no stock markets, no nuclear weapons, and their women did all the work. What could be more superior than that?

SUPERSTITIOUS

Burglar: The police are coming! Quick, jump out the window!
Accomplice: But we're on the thirteenth floor!
Burglar: This is no time to be superstitious.

SURFER

Man-over-board.

SURLY

Cheerful people, the doctors say, resist disease better than the glum ones. In other words, the surly bird catches the germ.

SURRENDER

Another word for engagement.

SUSPICIOUS CHARACTER

A man who suspects everybody.

SWEATER

A garment worn by a small child when his mother feels chilly.

Sweet Dreams

Q: Why did Clarence sprinkle sugar all over his pillow?
A: He wanted to have sweet dreams.

Swimming

I learned how to swim the old way when I was about five years old. My dad took me out to the middle of a lake in a boat and then threw me into the water. The swim back to shore was not too bad . . . it was getting out of the gunny sack.

Sympathy

Sympathy is what one girl offers another in exchange for details.

Synonym

"Johnny, what is a synonym?"
"A synonym is a word you use when you can't spell the word you want."

T

Tact

At a reception in Washington, a young man was asked by a widow to guess her age. "You must have some idea," she said, as he hesitated.

"I have several ideas," he admitted, with a smile. "The trouble is that I hesitate whether to make it ten years younger on account of your looks or ten years older on account of your intelligence."

⁓

Tact is the ability to make your guests feel at home when you wish they were.

⁓

What you don't say when you're angry.

Tailor

Customer: I'm sorry, but I won't be able to pay for this suit for two months.

Tailor: Oh, that's all right.

Customer: When will it be ready?

Tailor: In two months.

Talk

Talk is cheap because the supply is greater than the demand.

⁓

"You say there was something in her speech that sounded strange. What was that?"

"A pause."

⁓

"I don't think success has gone to her head."
"No, just to her mouth."

⚘ — ⚘

Son: Why do the ladies always bring their knitting when they come to visit?
Father: So they will have something to think about while they talk.

⚘ — ⚘

A great talker may be no fool, but he is one who relies on him.

⚘ — ⚘

Two great talkers will not travel far together.

⚘ — ⚘

Long talking begets short hearing.

⚘ — ⚘

The other day I was driving under the influence of my husband. He talks and talks. He gets two thousand words to the gallon.

TANTRUM

Teenager: Can I call you back in around fifteen minutes? I can't talk now; I'm in the middle of a tantrum.

⚘ — ⚘

The orchestra leader kept throwing tempo tantrums.

Tasks

Some tasks have to be put off dozens of times before they will completely slip your mind.

Taxes

A place with a lot of cowboys.

∽⊙—⊙∾

The income tax has made more liars out of the American people than gold has.
—*Will Rogers*

∽⊙—⊙∾

What is the difference between a taxidermist and a tax collector? The taxidermist takes only your skin.
—*Mark Twain*

∽⊙—⊙∾

The tax collector must love poor people—he's creating so many of them.

∽⊙—⊙∾

Nothing makes time pass more quickly than an income tax installment every three months.

∽⊙—⊙∾

"What would be a good way to raise revenue and still benefit the people?"
"Tax every political speech."

∽⊙—⊙∾

The reward for saving your money is being able to pay your taxes without borrowing.

∽⊖—⊖∾

An American can consider himself a success when it costs him more to support the government than to support a wife and children.

∽⊖—⊖∾

It's awfully difficult to believe that only about two hundred years ago we went to war to avoid taxation.

∽⊖—⊖∾

I'm gonna put all my money into taxes. They're sure to go up.

∽⊖—⊖∾

Income tax song: "Everything I Have Is Yours."

Taxi

A man had ridden three miles in a taxi when he suddenly realized he had left his wallet at home. He leaned forward and told the driver: "Stop at the drugstore for a minute. I want to get some matches so I can look for a twenty-dollar bill I've lost back here."

When he came out of the drugstore, the taxi had disappeared.

Taxpayers

People who don't have to take a civil service test to work for the government.

Tea

Three Englishmen stopped at a restaurant for a spot of tea. The waiter appeared with pad and pencil.

"I'll have a glass of weak tea," ordered the first.

"I'll have tea, too," said the second, "but very strong with two pieces of lemon."

"Tea for me, too, please," said the third. "But be sure the glass is absolutely clean."

In a short time the waiter was back with the order. "All right," he asked. "Which one gets the clean glass?"

TEACHER

Teacher: What do you call a person who keeps on talking when people are no longer interested?

Student: A teacher.

Not only is he the worst-behaved child in my class, but he also has a perfect attendance record!

A wise schoolteacher sends this note to all parents on the first day of school: "If you promise not to believe everything your child says happens at school, I'll promise not to believe everything he says happens at home."

TEAMWORK

Panting and perspiring, two men on a tandem bicycle at last got to the top of a steep hill.

"That was a stiff climb," said the first man.

"It certainly was," replied the second man. "And if I hadn't kept the brake on, we would have slid down backward."

TEARS

The world's greatest waterpower—women's tears.

Teenager

Father: Operator, I have been trying to reach my home for an hour and the line is busy. Could you please cut in on the line?

Operator: We can only cut in when it is a case of life or death.

Father: Well, I can tell you this much—if it's my teenage daughter on the phone, there's going to be a murder!

❦

The best substitute for experience is being sixteen.

❦

God is very providential. He gives us twelve years to develop a love for our children before turning them into teenagers.

❦

Father to teenage son: Do you mind if I use the car tonight? I'm taking your mother out and I would like to impress her.

❦

I never met a teenager who didn't get hungry from eating.

❦

My teenager finally found his stereo headphones that he's been looking for all winter. He got a haircut.

❦

Today's teenagers are on the phone so much, they don't even start talking until they hear a dial tone.

❦

Girl answering telephone: Judy isn't in just now. This is her 111–pound, five-foot-three, blonde, blue-eyed sister.

❦

Homework is something teenagers do between phone calls.

❦

The telephone is a remarkable invention. It allows teenagers to go steady without being able to hold hands.

❦

Why can't life's problems hit us when we're eighteen and know everything?

❦

My teenage daughter is at the stage where she's all skin and phones.

❦

If you want to recapture your youth, cut off his allowance.

❦

"Here is something that will make you feel really grown up," a father said to his daughter. "Your own phone bill."

❦

Teenagers are people you pay an allowance to for the privilege of living with them.

❦

A babysitter is a teenager who gets two dollars an hour to eat ten dollars worth of food.

❦

Teenagers complain there's nothing to do, then stay out all night doing it.

❦

"What did your teenage daughter do all summer?"
"Her hair and her nails!"

❧——☙

Oh, to be only half as wonderful as my child thought I was. And only half as stupid as my teenager thinks I am.

❧——☙

Father to teenage daughter: "I want you home by 11:00."
"But Daddy, I'm no longer a child."
"I know, that's why I want you home by 11:00."

Telepathy

A disease that you get from talking on the phone too much.

Temptation

A driver tucked this note under the windshield wiper of his automobile: "I've circled the block for twenty minutes. I'm late for an appointment and if I don't park here I'll lose my job. 'Forgive us our trespasses.'"
When he came back he found a parking ticket and this note: "I've circled the block for twenty years and if I don't give you a ticket, I'll lose my job. 'Lead us not into temptation.'"

Tenant

Tenant: I want you to get rid of the mice in my apartment.
Landlord: Not me . . . if they don't like it here, let them move.

Tender

Q: Why did the locomotive refuse to sit?
A: Because it had a tender behind.

TENURE

The number following nineure.

TERMITES

Dan: What do termites do when they want to relax?
Stan: They take a coffee-table break.

❧

The only thing that keeps my house from falling down is that the termites are holding hands.

TEXAN

Did you hear about the Texan who was trying to make a phone call?
"Operator, how much does it cost to call New York?"
"Three dollars and seventy-five cents," replied the operator.
"Why, I can call hell and back for that much," said the Texan.
"Yes, sir," said the operator, "that's a local call!"

❧

An ardent fisherman from Dallas made a trip to Bull Shoals Lake in Arkansas. After pulling in a 6 1/2 pound largemouth bass, the Texan boasted to his native guide, "Why, heck, in Texas we use that size for bait."
The Arkansan smiled, nodded appreciatively—and dropped the fish back into the lake.

❧

On a visit to tiny Israel, a Texan boasted, "Why, in Texas you can get on a train, ride for days, and still be in Texas."
His Israeli companion nodded sympathetically.
"We have the same trouble with our trains," he said.

❧

When you find a pair of boots on the floor with a big ten-gallon hat on top of them, what have you got? A Texan with all the hot air let out of him.

❦

A Texan was visiting Scotland, and every time his host would show him a sight he would say, "That's nothing! We've got the same thing in Texas, only better!"

Finally they arrived at Loch Lomond. The Texan said, "Well, you have one thing that we don't have in Texas. This is a pretty lake."

The host said, "Well, you could dig a pipeline from Texas under the ocean and into the lake. If you can suck as hard as you can blow, the lake is yours."

TEXT

That which ministers preach from, and often vary far from.

THANK YOU

Son: Dad, guess what? I can say please and thank you in Spanish.
Father: That's more than you ever learned to say in English.

THE END

A man was walking down some stairs when all of a sudden he slipped. In the process a stout lady toppled against him and they ended up on the bottom step with the lady sitting in the man's lap. The man tapped the lady on the shoulder. "I'm sorry, lady," he rasped, "but this is as far as I go."

THINK

The less a man thinks, the more he talks.

❦

The reason some of us find it difficult to think is that we haven't had any previous experience.

❦

There are two kinds of thinkers in the world. Those who think they can and those who think they can't . . . and they're both right.

Thirsty

Pete: I had an operation and the doctor left a sponge in me.
Bill: Got any pain?
Pete: No, but boy do I get thirsty.

Thoughtful

A very tight man was looking for a gift for a friend. Everything was too expensive except for a glass vase that had been broken, which he could purchase for almost nothing. He asked the store to send it, hoping his friend would think it had been broken in transit.

In due time, he received an acknowledgment. "Thanks for the vase," it read. "It was so thoughtful of you to wrap each piece separately."

Three Feet

"I've got a brother with three feet."
"What do you mean?"
"Well, my mother got a letter from my brother and he said, 'You would hardly know me—I've grown three feet.'"

Thumb-Sucker

A little boy was in the habit of sucking his thumb all the time. His mother tried everything to break him of the habit. Finally, one day she pointed to a fat man with a very large stomach and said that the man had grown his big stomach because he did not stop sucking his thumb.

The next day the child was with his mother in a supermarket, and he kept staring at a woman with a stomach that was obviously not at all normal. In fact the woman was very pregnant.

Finally the annoyed woman said to the child, "Stop staring at me like that. You don't know who I am."

"No," said the boy, "but I know what you have been doing."

Tight

He's so tight he keeps five-dollar bills folded so long that Lincoln gets ingrown whiskers.

Tip

Customer: I am sorry, waiter, but I only have enough money for the bill. I have nothing left for a tip.

Waiter: Let me add up that bill again, sir.

⊷⊶

I hate to always eat and run, but the way I tip, it's the only safe procedure.

Toe

Nothing is harder to do secretly than stub your toe.

Tolerance

Tolerance is the uncomfortable suspicion that the person you're talking to may be right.

⊷⊶

Tolerance is the art of putting up with people who aren't perfect like you.

Tomorrow

Ken: There's nothing like getting up at five in the morning and taking an ice-cold shower and a five-mile jog before breakfast.
Bob: How long have you been doing this?
Ken: I start tomorrow.

Tongue

The tongue is a wet place, and easily slips.

∽⊖—⊖∾

A sharp tongue is the only edge tool that grows keener with constant use.
—*Washington Irving*

∽⊖—⊖∾

Don't let your tongue say what your head may pay for.

∽⊖—⊖∾

He who has a sharp tongue usually cuts his own throat.

Tongue Twisters

Six shy soldiers sold seven salted salmons.

∽⊖—⊖∾

Two tree toads tied together tried to trot to town twice.

∽⊖—⊖∾

Bisquick, kiss quick.

∽⊖—⊖∾

Six slippery, sliding snakes.

❦

Fat friars fanning flames.

❦

Jack Jackson Zachary.

❦

The judge judged Judd.

❦

Three terrible thieves.

❦

Tim, the thin twin tinsmith.

❦

Strange strategic statistics.

❦

Toy boat.

❦

Six slick saplings.

Too Long

The master of ceremonies got up to close the meeting after a very long-winded speaker. "You have just been listening to that famous Chinese statesman, On Too Long."

Toothache

There was never yet a philosopher
That could endure the toothache patiently.
—*Shakespeare*

Tough Neighborhood

My neighborhood was so bad that even the police station had a peephole in the front door.

◦◦○—◦◦

My neighborhood was so bad that our school newspaper had an obituary page.

◦◦○—◦◦

I don't want to say that I live in a bad neighborhood, but the criminals are so tough that they attack people with chewed-off shotguns.

Traffic Fine

"What am I supposed to do with this?" grumbled the motorist as the police clerk handed him a receipt for his traffic fine.
"Keep it," the clerk advised. "When you get four of these, you get a bicycle."

Traffic Jam

A substance for spreading on streets at five o'clock.

Train

Porter: Did you miss that train, sir?
Man: No! I didn't like the looks of it, so I chased it out of the station.

◦◦○—◦◦

Buck: Did you ever wonder why there are so many more auto wrecks than railway accidents?

Bill: Did you ever hear of the fireman hugging the engineer?

∾⊝—⊝∾

Two elderly women on a commuter train got into an argument about the window: One insisted that it had to be open or she would suffocate; the other demanded that it be closed so she would not catch a cold. The conductor was asked to settle the noisy dispute.

A commuter nearby called to the conductor, "Open the window first, and let one of them catch cold and die. Then close it and let the other one suffocate."

TRAMP

Lady: You should be ashamed to ask for handouts in this neighborhood.

Tramp: Don't apologize for it, ma'am. I've seen worse.

TRANQUILIZER

Lately he's tried tranquilizers to reduce. He hasn't lost any weight, but he has stopped worrying about being beefy and paunchy.

TRICKLE

Teacher: What does trickle mean?

Student one: To run slowly.

Teacher: Good. And what does anecdote mean?

Student two: It's a short, funny tale.

Teacher: Well done. Now, give me a sentence with both of those word in it.

Student three: Our dog trickled down the street wagging her anecdote.

TRICYCLE

A tot rod.

Trouble

A few years ago a friend was in trouble and I helped him out. "I won't forget you," he vowed. And he didn't. He's in trouble again and just called me.

❧—❧

Professor: Name a product in which the supply always exceeds the demand.
Student: Trouble.

Truck Driving

Two truck drivers applied for a job. One said, "I'm Pete and this is my partner, Mike. When I drive at night, he sleeps."

The man said, "All right, I'll give you an oral test. It's three o'clock in the morning. You're on a little bridge and your truck is loaded with nitroglycerin. All of a sudden a truck comes toward you at about eighty miles per hour. What's the first thing you do?"

"I wake up my partner, Mike—he never saw a wreck like this before."

Trumpet

A man mentioned to his landlord about the tenants in the apartment over his. "Many a night they stamp on the floor and shout till midnight."

When the landlord asked if it bothered him, he replied, "Not really, for I usually stay up and practice my trumpet till about that time most every night anyway."

Trust

In God we trust—all others pay cash.

❧—❧

I would trust other people more if I knew myself less.

❧—❧

Judge: How could you swindle these good people who trusted you so?
Con man: Your Honor, you can't swindle people who don't trust you.

Truthfulness

There's no limit to the height a man can attain by remaining on the level.

Try Again

Off the coast of Oregon, a ship collided with a fishing boat in heavy fog. No real damage was done, but as the offending ship tried to back off, it banged into the boat again. The captain was afraid he might have done some damage with the second blow. "Can you stay afloat?" he shouted through a megaphone to the floundering victim.

"I guess so," called back the skipper of the boat. "Do you want to try again?"

Tulips

The standard number of lips assigned to each person.

TV Dinner

"One more TV dinner and you'll be looking for a new sponsor."

⧯

I know a woman who has cooked so many TV dinners she thinks she's in show business.

Twentieth Century

A man put a coin in a vending machine and watched helplessly while the cup failed to appear. One nozzle sent coffee down the drain while another poured cream after it.

"Now that's real automation!" he exclaimed. "It even drinks for you!"

❦

Watching the television news, we find that our highways aren't safe, our streets aren't safe, our parks aren't safe . . . but under our arms we've got complete protection.

❦

The man of the twentieth century is one who drives a mortgaged car over a bond-financed highway on credit-card gas.

Twins

Instant replay.

❦

Insult added to injury.

Two-Faced

Once during a debate Lincoln was accused by Douglas of being two-faced. Without hesitation, Lincoln calmly replied, "I leave it to my audience . . . if I had two faces, would I be wearing this one?"

Typewriter

"I operate a typewriter by the biblical system."
"What is that?"
"The 'seek-and-ye-shall-find' system."

⊰ U ⊱

Ugly

Tell me, is that your lower lip, or are you wearing a turtleneck sweater?

⤳⊙—⊙⤳

She has long, flowing blonde hair . . . from each nostril.

⤳⊙—⊙⤳

With those varicose veins, she could win first prize at a costume party by going as a road map.

⤳⊙—⊙⤳

Judy: What did you do to your hair? It looks like a wig.
Joan: It is a wig.
Judy: You know? You could never tell!

⤳⊙—⊙⤳

"Your face would stop a clock."
"And yours would make one run!"

⤳⊙—⊙⤳

In appearance, I'm not a guest star,
Others are handsomer—far.
But my face—I don't mind it
Because I'm behind it;
It's the poor folks out front that I jar.

⤳⊙—⊙⤳

Jean: Do you think she is a natural blonde or a bleached blonde?
Zona: I think she's a suicide blonde.

Jean: What kind is that?
Zona: Dyed by her own hand.

⌒⊙—⊙⌒

Her nostrils are so big that when you kiss her it's like driving into a two-car garage.

⌒⊙—⊙⌒

"My wife spent four hours in the beauty shop the other day."
"Boy, that's a long time."
"Yeah, and that was just for the estimate!"

ULCER

An ulcer is what you get mountain-climbing over molehills.

UMPIRE

Wife: John, what becomes of a ball player when his eyesight starts to fail?
John: They make an umpire of him.

UNAWARE

Q: What is the meaning of the word "unaware"?
A: Unaware is what you put on first and take off last.

UNBALANCED

They say that one in every four Americans is unbalanced. Think of your three closest friends. If they seem okay, then you're in trouble.

Underwear

Something that creeps up on you.

Union

Man filling out an application for union membership: "Does this union have any death benefits?"

"Sure does," replied the union representative. "When you die you don't have to pay any more dues."

❀

Unions are getting such a bad name, it's no wonder they're called Brother Hoods.

University

Universities are full of knowledge; the freshmen bring a little in and the seniors take none away, and knowledge accumulates.

❀

An institution for the postponement of experience.

Unkempt

A guy goes to the doctor and the doctor says, "You have the dirtiest, most unkempt, uncivilized body I have ever seen."

The patient says, "That's funny, that's what the other doctor told me yesterday."

"Then," asks the doctor, "why did you come to see me?"

The patient answers, "I wanted a second opinion."

Untouchables

People as broke as we are.

Upper Crust

A lot of crumbs held together by dough.

ᗕ V ᗏ

VACATION

A period of travel and relaxation when you take twice the clothes and half the money you need.

∾⊖—⊖∾

No man needs a vacation so much as the man who has just had one.

∾⊖—⊖∾

A vacation resort is where you go when you are worn out and where you come back from a complete wreck.

∾⊖—⊖∾

The bigger the summer vacation the harder the fall.

∾⊖—⊖∾

Husband to wife: Well, in a way it's a two-week vacation . . . I take a week and then the boss takes a week.

VALUE

If a man empties his purse into his head, no one can take it from him.
—*Benjamin Franklin*

VEIL

A minister married a couple. The woman had on a veil and he could not see her face. After the ceremony, the man asked the minister, "How much do I owe you?"

"No charge," replied the minister.

"But I want to show my appreciation." So the man gave him fifty cents.

About that time the bride pulled off her veil, and the minister, looking at the bride, gave the man twenty-five cents change.

VETERINARIAN

A rancher asked a veterinarian for some free advice. "I have a horse that walks normally sometimes, and sometimes he limps. What shall I do?"

The veterinarian replied, "The next time he walks normally, sell him."

VINEGAR

A Boy Scout was out trying to raise funds for his troop by collecting bottles and cans. He went to one house and asked the lady if she had any old beer bottles.

The self-righteous woman retorted, "Do I look like the kind of person who would drink beer?"

"Pardon me," apologized the Boy Scout. "Do you have any old vinegar bottles?"

VISION

One may have good eyes, and see nothing.

∽✑—✑∼

Don't call the world dirty because you have forgotten to clean your glasses.

∽✑—✑∼

Did you hear about the spinster who could not see too well? In order to hide her failing eyesight from her intended, she stuck a pin in a tree. The next day, while walking in the forest with him, she pointed to the tree, some hundred yards distant, and said, "Isn't that a pin sticking in that tree?" And as she ran to retrieve it, she tripped over a cow.

Voting

A man walked up to a farmer as he came out of a voting booth and said, "I'm from the FBI."

"What seems to be the trouble?"

"We happen to know that you accepted a bribe and sold your vote."

"That's not true. I voted for the candidate because I like him."

"Well, that's where we've got you. We have concrete evidence you accepted fifty dollars from him."

"Well, it's plain common sense. If someone gives you fifty dollars, you're going to like him."

⇥ W ⇤

Waiter, Oh, Waiter!

Diner: Is it customary to tip the waiter in this restaurant?
Waiter: Why . . . ah . . . yes, sir.
Diner: Then hand me a tip. I've waited almost an hour for that steak I ordered.

A waiter is one who believes that money grows on trays.

Waiter: May I help you with that soup, sir?
Sailor: What do you mean, help me? I don't need any help.
Waiter: Sorry. From the sound I thought you might wish to be dragged ashore.

Diner: Waiter, please close the window.
Waiter: Is there is draft, sir?
Diner: Yes, it's the third time my steak has blown off the plate!

Customer: I'll have some raw oysters, not too large nor too small, not too salty nor too fat. They must be cold and I want them quickly!
Waiter: Yes, sir! With or without pearls?

Customer: Would you mind taking the fly out of my soup?
Waiter: Do it yourself. I'm no lifeguard.

Customer: This coffee tastes like mud.
Waiter: Well, it was ground this morning.

❦

Man: There's a splinter in my cottage cheese!
Waiter: What do you expect for fifty-five cents . . . the whole cottage?

❦

Customer: Waiter! There's a fly in my soup!
Waiter: Don't worry, sir, the spider in the bread will get it.

❦

Customer: Waiter! There's a fly in my soup!
Waiter: Okay, here's a flyswatter.

❦

Customer: Waiter! There's a fly in my soup!
Waiter: Just a moment, sir—I'll get some fly spray.

❦

Customer: Waiter! There's a fly in my soup!
Waiter: Now there's a fly that knows good soup.

❦

Customer: Waiter! There's a fly in my soup!
Waiter: Go ahead and eat him; there's more where he came from.

❦

Customer: Waiter! There's a fly in my soup!
Waiter: Just wait until you see the main course.

❦

Customer: Waiter! There's a fly in my soup!
Waiter: Yes, sir, better sip it with care.

∽◦—◦∾

Customer: Waiter! There's a fly in my soup!
Waiter: Serves the chef right. I told him not to strain the broth through the flyswatter.

∽◦—◦∾

Customer: Waiter! There's a fly in my soup!
Waiter: That's funny. There were two of them when I left the kitchen.

∽◦—◦∾

Customer: Waiter! There's a fly in my soup!
Waiter: Half a fly would be worse.

∽◦—◦∾

Customer: Waiter! There's a fly in my soup!
Waiter: Shhhhhhh! Everyone will want one.

∽◦ ◦∾

Customer: Waiter! What's this fly doing in my soup!
Waiter: Dunno, sir. It looks like the backstroke to me.

∽◦—◦∾

Customer: Waiter! There's a dead fly swimming in my soup!
Waiter: Nonsense, sir. Dead flies can't swim.

∽◦—◦∾

Customer: Waiter! There's a fly in my applesauce!
Waiter: Of course, sir. It's a fruit fly.

∽◦—◦∾

Customer: Waiter! What's this cockroach doing in my soup?
Waiter: We ran out of flies.

⌁

Customer: Waiter! There's a twig in my soup!
Waiter: Sorry, sir. I'll go get the branch manager.

WAITING ROOM

People who think that time heals everything haven't tried sitting it out in a doctor's waiting room.

⌁

Every chair in the doctor's waiting room was filled and some patients were standing. At one point the conversation died down and there was silence. During the silence an old man stood up wearily and remarked, "Well, guess I'll go home and die a natural death."

WAR

Another thing against war is that it seldom if ever kills off the right people.

WARDROBE

The Law of the Wardrobe:

Daring	1 year before its time
Chic	in its time
Dowdy	3 years after its time
Hideous	20 years after its time
Amusing	30 years after its time
Romantic	100 years after its time
Beautiful	150 years after its time

Watch

First man: I got my wife a lady's wristwatch.
Second man: Did she like it?
First man: Yes, but the lady came and took it back.

Watermelons

Fruit and vegetable market: Best watermelons you ever seed.

⧽—⧼

Two watermelons cannot be held under one arm.

Wavelength

The distance from the scalp to the end of the curl.

Weather

Don't knock the weather; nine-tenths of the people couldn't start a conversation if it didn't change once in a while.

⧽—⧼

Everybody talks about the weather but nobody does anything about it.

Wedding

Did you hear about the married man who ran his wedding movies backward . . . he wanted to remember what it was like to be a free man.

⧽—⧼

"I hear the groom ran away from the altar."
"Lost his nerve, I suppose?"
"No, found it again."

WEDDING RING

A one-man band.

WEEVILS

Two boll weevils came from the country to the city. One became rich and famous. The other remained the lesser of the two weevils.

WEIGHT

Some women would be more spic if they had less span.

❧

Doctors tell us there are over seven million people who are overweight. These, of course, are only round figures.

❧

It's not the minutes you spend at the table that make you fat—it's the seconds.

❧

There's a reducing salon on Wall Street for stocky brokers.

❧

I fell asleep on a beach and burned my stomach. You should see my pot roast!

❧

You can't reduce by talking about reducing. It's better to keep your mouth shut.

WELFARE

Protester to his girlfriend: I'm on my way to pick up my unemployment check. Then I'll go over to the university office to see what's holding up this month's Federal Education Grant. Then I'll go and get this week's food stamps. Meanwhile you can go over to the Free Health Clinic and check up on your tests. I've got to drop around at the Welfare Department and demand our eligibility limit again. Then at 4:00 P.M. we'll meet at the Federal Building for another mass demonstration against this stinking, rotten establishment.

WELL-DEVELOPED

Lucy: What well-developed arms you have.
Betty: Yes, I play a lot of tennis.
Lucy: You ride horseback, too, don't you?

WHALE SANDWICH

Customer: Your sign says, "Any sandwich you can name." I would like a whale sandwich."
Waiter: Okay. (Disappears into kitchen and shortly returns.) I'm afraid I can't get you a whale sandwich.
Customer: Why not? Your sign says "any sandwich."
Waiter: The cook says he doesn't want to start a new whale for one lousy sandwich.

WHAT A TAIL

A man walked by a table in a hotel and noticed three men and a dog playing cards. The dog was giving an extraordinary performance.
"This is a very smart dog," the man commented.

"Not so smart," said one of the players. "Every time he gets a good hand he wags his tail."

Wheelbarrows

One day a fellow started through the gate of a large factory wheeling a wheelbarrow full of sawdust and was stopped by the guard. He told the guard he had permission to take the sawdust out of the factory.

The guard checked and found out that this was correct, and so he let the fellow go on his way. This same thing continued for many days thereafter.

Finally, a fellow worker asked the sawdust collector what he was up to. "Are you stealing all this sawdust, or what?"

"No," was the reply, "Not sawdust—I'm stealing wheelbarrows."

Whim

The plural of whim is women.

Whisper

Some people believe everything you tell them—especially if you whisper it.

Whistle

Mark: I'll bet you're one of those people who drop their work and beat it as soon as the 5:00 P.M. whistle blows.

Clark: Not me. After I quit work I usually wait about ten minutes for the whistle to blow.

Whole Load

One Sunday a farmer went to church. When he entered he saw that he and the preacher were the only ones present. The preacher asked the farmer if he wanted him to go ahead and preach. The farmer said, "I'm not too smart, but if I went to feed my cattle and only one showed up, I'd feed him." So the minister began his sermon.

One hour passed, then two hours, then two-and-a-half hours. The preacher finally finished and came down to ask the farmer how he had liked the sermon.

The farmer answered slowly, "Well, I'm not very smart, but if I went to feed my cattle and only one showed up, I sure wouldn't feed him all the hay."

WHO'S DYING?

An immigrant who worked his way up to the biggest fleet of push-carts in the world knew he was dying and decided to face up to things. He therefore called an attorney to his bedside, and, after ordering his wife not to cry, started to dispose of his worldly possessions.

"My Cadillac with the push-button motorcycle cop detector I leave to my son, George."

"Better you should leave it to Joe," Bertha interrupted. "He's a better driver."

"So let it be Joe," he whispered. "My Rolls Royce with the specially constructed Ford hot-rod engine I bequeath to my daughter, Linda."

"You had better give it to your nephew, Willie," Bertha again interrupted. "He's a very conservative driver."

"All right, give it to Willie. My twelve-cylinder Volvo I give to my niece, Sally."

"Personally, I think Judy should get it."

Unable to take any more, he raised his head from the pillow and shouted, "Bertha, please, who's dying? You or me?"

WIFE

Any wife with an inferiority complex can cure it by being sick in bed for a day while her husband manages the household and the children.

❧ — ❧

Nobody can cook like my wife, Joan, but they came pretty close to it when I was in the Army.

❧ — ❧

First husband: Last night my wife dreamed she was married to a millionaire.

Second husband: You're lucky. My wife thinks that in the daytime.

Wig

Now there's a wig to wear to the supermarket. It has curlers in it.

Will

A dead giveaway.

∽᙮−᙮∾

Lawyer, reading a wise old man's will to the relatives: And being of sound mind, I spent every dollar I had.

∽᙮−᙮∾

A rich uncle died and a line in his will read as follows: I leave to my beloved nephew all the money he owes me.

Wind

No wind is a good wind if you don't know where the harbor is.

∽᙮−᙮∾

A tourist traveling through western Kansas saw a man sitting by the ruins of a house that had been blown away.

"Was this your house, my friend?" he asked sympathetically.

"Yep."

"Any of your family blown away with the house?"

"Yep, wife and four kids."

"Great Scot, man, why aren't you hunting for them?"

"Well, stranger, I've been in this country quite a spell. The wind's due to change this afternoon. So I figure I might as well wait here till it brings 'em back."

∽᙮−᙮∾

Two farmers were boasting about the strongest wind they'd seen.

"In California," said one, "I've seen the fiercest wind in my life. You know those giant redwood trees? Well, the wind once got so strong that it bent them right over."

"That's nothing," said the other. "Back on my farm in Iowa, we had a terrible wind one day that blew a hundred miles per hour. It was so bad, one of my hens had her back turned to the wind and she laid the same egg six times."

WINDOW-SHOPPER

A store gazer.

WINE-AGE

People are like wine—age sours the bad and improves the good.

WISE WIFE

A wise wife is one who asks for something she knows her husband can't afford so that she can compromise on what she really wants.

WISHY-WASHY

"I hate vague, noncommittal, middle-of-the-road people, don't you?"
"Mmmmmmmmm!"

WIT

A fellow who thinks he's a wit is usually half-right.

∽⧼–⧽∾

Wit is the salt of the conversation, not the food.

❦

The next best thing to being witty oneself is to be able to quote another's wit.

❦

He who has provoked the shaft of wit, cannot complain that he smarts from it.
—*Samuel Johnson*

❦

To be witty is not enough. One must possess sufficient wit to avoid having too much of it.

❦

Wit is not always grinning.

❦

Wit without wisdom is salt without meat.

❦

All wit is not wisdom.

❦

Wit without discretion is a sword in the hand of a fool.

WOMAN

Creature whom God made beautiful that man might love her, and unreasonable that she might love man.

❦

Woman was created after man and has been after him ever since.

❦

Any man who thinks he's more intelligent than his wife is married to a smart woman.

❦

A fallen woman is a mother whose children didn't pick up their toys.

❦

You see, dear, it is not true that woman was made from man's rib; she was really made from his funny bone.

❦

The way to fight a woman is with your hat. Grab it and run.
—*John Barrymore*

❦

Being a woman is a terribly difficult task since it consists principally in dealing with men.

Women's Lib

Adam-smasher.

❦

Women's libber: The time will come when women will get men's wages.
Husband in audience: So true, next payday.

❦

"For months," said a women's libber, "I couldn't imagine where my husband spent his evenings."

"And then what happened?" breathlessly asked her friend.

"Well," she said, "one evening I went home and there he was."

❧ ❧

With the Women's Lib movement coming in so strong, one cereal company had to change their advertisement to "*snap, crackle, mom.*"

❧ ❧

A Ms. is as good as a male.

WONDERFUL

"Has anyone ever told you how wonderful you are?"

"Nope."

"Well, then, where did you get the idea?"

❧ ❧

We have a strange and wonderful relationship. He's strange and I'm wonderful.

WOODEN LEG

Fred: There is a man outside with a wooden leg named Martin.

Jed: What is the name of his other leg?

Fred: I think it's Peg.

❧ ❧

Timmy: My grandfather has a wooden leg.

Jimmy: Well, my grandmother has a cedar chest.

WOOL

There was a man who owned a lot of sheep and wanted to take them over a river that was all ice, but the woman who owned the river said,

"No." So he promised to marry her and that's how he pulled the wool over her ice.

WORK

Don't bother to boast of your work to others; the work itself has a much better voice.

No bees, no honey;
No work, no money.

Pursue thy work without delay,
For the short hours run fast away.

Modern-day teenager to millionaire: "What's the first secret of your success?"
"Hard work."
"What's the second one?"

God gives every bird its food, but does not throw it into the nest.

Half the people like to work and the other half don't, or maybe it's the other way 'round.

Jim: It's no disgrace to work.
Tim: That's what I tell my wife.

Lady: Why don't you work? Hard work never killed anyone.
Bum: You're wrong, lady. I lost both of my wives that way.

◦⟋⊙——⊙⟍◦

Work is the yeast that raises the dough.

◦⟋⊙——⊙⟍◦

It's probably true that hard work is a tonic, but many people never get sick enough to try the remedy.

◦⟋⊙——⊙⟍◦

Father: Why don't you get yourself a job?
Son: Why?
Father: So you could earn some money.
Son: Why?
Father: So you could put some money in a bank account and earn interest.
Son: Why?
Father: So that when you're old you can use the money in your bank account . . . and you would never have to work again.
Son: I'm not working now.

◦⟋⊙——⊙⟍◦

Boss: Jones, how long have you been working here?
Jones: Ever since I heard you coming down the hall.

◦⟋⊙——⊙⟍◦

Boss: I notice you go out and get your hair cut during business hours.
Employee: My hair grows during business hours.
Boss: But it doesn't all grow during business hours.
Employee: I didn't get it all cut.

◦⟋⊙——⊙⟍◦

First employee: How long have you been working here?
Second employee: Ever since the day the foreman threatened to fire me.

◦⊙—⊙◦

By working faithfully eight hours a day, you may eventually get to be a boss and work twelve hours a day.

◦⊙—⊙◦

Some people are like blisters. They don't show up until the work is finished.

◦⊙—⊙◦

Visitor: How many people work here in your plant?
Manager: Oh, about one out of ten!

◦⊙—⊙◦

Politician: What we need is a working majority.
Merchant: What we really need is a majority working.

◦⊙—⊙◦

"Here's one name on the committee that I never heard of."
"Oh, that's probably the person who actually does the work."

◦⊙—⊙◦

Boss to new employee: Most amazing; you've been with us two weeks and already you're a month behind in your work.

◦⊙—⊙◦

Boss: You should have been here at eight o'clock this morning.
Secretary: Why? What happened?

◦⊙—⊙◦

Teach your son to cut his own wood. It will warm him twice.

❦—❦

Boss: Have you anything to say before I fire you?
Employee: Yes. How about a raise?

❦—❦

"I'm really not late, boss, I just took my coffee break before coming in."

❦—❦

Employer: Why do you ask for a raise?
Employee: Sir, I wouldn't ask you for a raise, but somehow my kids found out that other families eat three times a day.

❦—❦

Salesman to customer: This is actually a fire sale. The boss said that if I don't make a sale, I'm fired.

❦—❦

One unemployed man to another: What hurts was that I wasn't replaced by a whole computer—just a transistor.

❦—❦

First girl: I lost my job because of illness and fatigue.
Second girl: That's too bad.
First girl: Yeah, my boss got sick and tired of me.

❦—❦

Personnel man to trainee: Or if you prefer, you may elect to skip coffee breaks entirely and retire three years early.

❦—❦

Employee: Sir, I've been with you for twenty-seven years, and I've never before asked for a raise.

Boss: That's why you've been with me for twenty-seven years.

WORLD

A big ball that revolves on its taxes.

WORLD'S CHAMPIONSHIP

"I remember my wedding day very distinctly," said the elderly gentleman. "I carried my new bride across the threshold of our little house and said, 'Honey, this is your and my little world.'"

"And I suppose you've lived happily ever after?"

"We've been fighting for the world's championship ever since."

WORRY

Worry is interest paid on trouble before it is due.

✧

Don't tell me that worry doesn't do any good. I know better. The things I worry about don't happen.

✧

Worry gives a small thing a big shadow.

✧

The reason why worry kills more people than work is that more people worry than work.

—*Robert Frost*

✧

I am an old man and have known a great many troubles, but most of them never happened.
—*Mark Twain*

∽⊙—⊙∾

To worry about tomorrow is to be unhappy today.

∽⊙—⊙∾

To carry care to bed is to sleep with a pack on your back.

∽⊙—⊙∾

There are two days about which nobody should ever worry, and these are yesterday and tomorrow.

∽⊙—⊙∾

Worry grows lushly in the soil of its sorrow; it only saps today of its joy.

∽⊙—⊙∾

We probably wouldn't worry about what people think of us if we could know how seldom they do.

∽⊙—⊙∾

The greatest fool is he who worries about what he cannot help.

WRINKLE-PROOF

An affidavit stating that you have wrinkles.

WRINKLES

If you would keep the wrinkles out of your face, keep sunshine in your heart.

WRITER

Writer: Have you read my latest joke book?
Friend: No, I only read for pleasure or profit.

※ ⁃⊖— ⊝⁃

Writer: Have you read my latest joke book?
Friend: Not yet. But I shall lose no time reading it.

※ ⁃⊖— ⊝⁃

Writer: Have you read my latest joke book?
Friend: No. But I have no doubt that your joke book will fill a much-needed void.

※ ⁃⊖— ⊝⁃

Writer: Just think . . . my parents didn't want me to become a well-known author.
Friend: I guess they got their wish.

※ ⁃⊖— ⊝⁃

"Mr. Editor, do you think I should put more fire into my stories?"
"No, just the opposite."

WRITER'S CRAMP

Authoritis.

WRONG AGAIN

Husband: We have been married for five years and haven't agreed on a thing.
Wife: You're wrong again—it's been six years.

X-Ray

Belly vision.

Y

You Asked For It

"Doctor," she said loudly, bouncing into the room, "I want you to say frankly what's wrong with me."

He surveyed her from head to foot. "Madam," he said at length, "I've just three things to tell you."

"First, your weight needs to be reduced by nearly sixty pounds.

"Second, your beauty would be improved if you used one-tenth as much rouge and lipstick.

"And, third, I'm an artist—the doctor lives on the next floor."

Young People

Young people are often bad because their parents did not burn their britches behind them.

⇥ Z ⇤

Zoo

A place devised for animals to study the strange habits of human beings.

⟡—⟡—⟡

An insurance agent was writing a policy for a zookeeper. "Have you ever had any accidents?"

"No," said the zookeeper. "But once a rattlesnake bit me and an elephant stepped on my foot."

"Don't you call those accidents?" asked the insurance agent.

"No," replied the zookeeper, "they did it on purpose."